Last Poems

BOOKS BY HAYDEN CARRUTH

POETRY

The Crow and the Heart: 1946–1959, Macmillan (New York, NY), 1959

In Memoriam: G. V. C., privately printed, 1960

Journey to a Known Place (long poem), New Directions (New York, NY), 1961

The Norfolk Poems: 1 June to 1 September 1961, Prairie Press (Iowa City, IA), 1962

North Winter, Prairie Press (Iowa City, IA), 1964

Nothing for Tigers: Poems, 1959–1964, Macmillan (New York, NY), 1965

Contra Mortem (long poem), Crow's Mark Press (Johnson, VT), 1967

For You: Poems, New Directions (New York, NY), 1970

The Clay Hill Anthology, Prairie Press (Iowa City, IA), 1970

From Snow and Rock, from Chaos: Poems, 1965–1972, New Directions (New York, NY), 1973

Dark World, Kayak (Santa Cruz, CA), 1974

The Bloomingdale Papers, University of Georgia Press (Athens, GA), 1975

Loneliness: An Outburst of Hexasyllables, Janus Press (Rogue River, OR), 1976

Aura, Janus Press (Rogue River, OR), 1977

Brothers, I Loved You All, Sheep Meadow (New York, NY), 1978

Almanach du Printemps Vivarois, Nadja (New York, NY), 1979

The Mythology of Dark and Light, Tamarack Press (Madison, WI), 1982

The Sleeping Beauty (long poem), Harper (New York, NY), 1982; revised edition, Copper Canyon Press (Port Townsend, WA), 1990

If You Call This Cry a Song, Countryman Press (Woodstock, VT), 1983

Asphalt Georgics, New Directions (New York, NY), 1985

Lighter Than Air Craft, Bucknell University Press (Lewisburg, PA), 1985

The Oldest Killed Lake in North America: Poems, 1979–1981, Salt-Works Press (Grenada, MS), 1985

Mother, Tamarack Press (Madison, WI), 1985

The Selected Poetry of Hayden Carruth, Macmillan (New York, NY), 1985

Sonnets, Press of Appletree Alley (Lewisburg, PA), 1989

Tell Me Again How the White Heron Rises and Flies Across the Nacreous River at Twilight Toward the Distant Islands, New Directions (New York, NY), 1989

Collected Shorter Poems, 1946–1991, Copper Canyon Press (Port Townsend, WA), 1992

Collected Longer Poems, Copper Canyon Press (Port Townsend, WA), 1994

Scrambled Eggs and Whiskey: Poems, 1991–1995, Copper Canyon Press (Port Townsend, WA), 1996

Doctor Jazz, Copper Canyon Press (Port Townsend, WA), 2001

Toward the Distant Islands: New and Selected Poems, Copper Canyon Press (Port Townsend, WA), 2006

Last Poems, Copper Canyon Press (Port Townsend, WA), 2012

OTHER

Appendix A (novel), Macmillan (New York, NY), 1963

After The Stranger: Imaginary Dialogues with Camus (novel), Macmillan (New York, NY), 1964

Working Papers: Selected Essays and Reviews, edited by Judith Weissman, University of Georgia Press (Athens, GA), 1981

Effluences from the Sacred Caves: More Selected Essays and Reviews, University of Michigan Press (Ann Arbor, MI), 1984

Sitting In: Selected Writings on Jazz, Blues, and Related Topics (includes poetry), University of Iowa Press (Iowa City, IA), 1986; expanded edition, 1993

Suicides and Jazzers, University of Michigan Press (Ann Arbor, MI), 1992

Selected Essays and Reviews, Copper Canyon Press (Port Townsend, WA), 1995

Reluctantly: Autobiographical Essays, Copper Canyon Press (Port Townsend, WA), 1998

Beside the Shadblow Tree: A Memoir of James Laughlin, Copper Canyon Press (Port Townsend, WA), 1999

Listener's Guide: Reading from Collected Shorter Poems *and* Scrambled Eggs and Whiskey (sound recording), Copper Canyon Press (Port Townsend, WA), 1999

Letters to Jane (correspondence), Ausable Press (Keene, NY), 2004

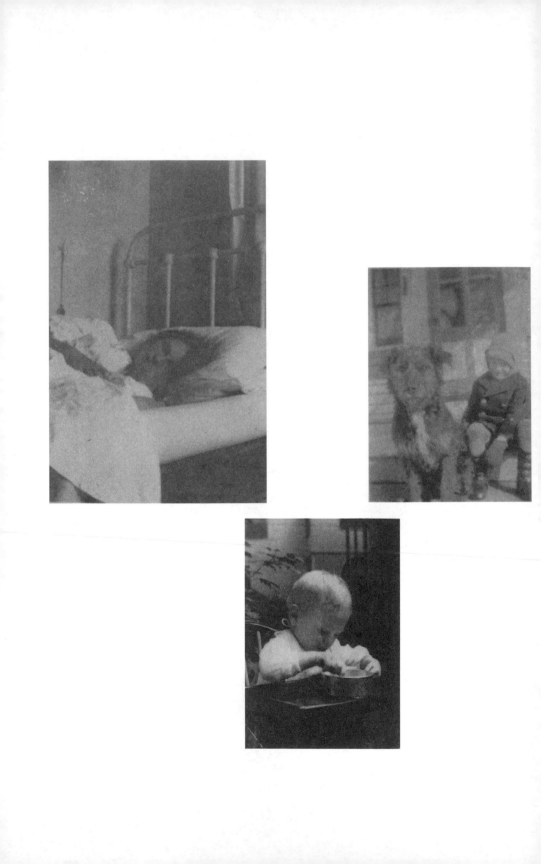

Hayden Carruth

Last Poems

COPPER CANYON PRESS

PORT TOWNSEND, WASHINGTON

Copper Canyon Press is in residence at Fort Worden State Park in Port Townsend,
Washington, under the auspices of Centrum. Centrum is a gathering place for
artists and creative thinkers from around the world, students of all ages and
backgrounds, and audiences seeking extraordinary cultural enrichment.

LIBRARY OF CONGRESS CATALOGING-IN-PUBLICATION DATA
Carruth, Hayden, 1921–2008
[Poems. Selections]
Last poems / Hayden Carruth, [Brooks Haxton, Stephen Dobyns]
p. cm.
ISBN 978–1–55659–381–9 (alk. paper)
I. Haxton, Brooks, 1950- II. Dobyns, Stephen, 1941- III. Title.
PS3505.A77594.A6 2012
811`.54—DC23
2011035175

FIRST PRINTING

COPPER CANYON PRESS
Post Office Box 271
Port Townsend, Washington 98368

www.coppercanyonpress.org

*With deepest gratitude to Dr. Laderman,
who gave his unflagging care and deepest attention
through the end of Hayden's days.*

CONTENTS

LAST POEMS

THE ACT OF LOVE: A PREFACE

Hayden Carruth's poetry as been foundational to Copper Canyon Press; his long poem *The Sleeping Beauty* was brought back into print in 1990 by our cofounding editor Sam Hamill, who would become one of Carruth's greatest advocates and dearest friends. With the subsequent publication of his *Collected Shorter Poems*, the bulk of Carruth's work was reintroduced and started to earn him the major awards and recognition that had passed him by for so much of his career. It would also introduce a younger generation of readers—myself included—to one of the twentieth century's most versatile, ethically uncompromising, and significant poets.

When Carruth passed away, in September 2008 at the age of eighty-seven, he left behind a number of poems and fragments—work unpublished after *Toward the Distant Islands* came out in 2006. When we considered these poems together with the thoughtful and intentional way he ended all his books, the idea emerged for a final book that would serve as an intimate retrospective and a public celebration of an international poetic treasure. As the book developed and synchronicities arose, we were surprised, haunted, and deeply humbled—the conviction, honesty, and clear-eyed existential acceptance that marked his sensibility are obvious throughout.

When compiling the last poems from previously published works, the primary editorial convention was to use the most recently revised work. But in the case of "Poetical Abstracts," we restored sections and stanzas that had been deleted from the *Shorter Poems*. For previously published book-length poems, we have printed only the last section; however, we have included here "Moon" and "Aura," poems that have been out of print for decades and that we now have the opportunity to reintroduce.

It is a bittersweet event to acknowledge a final manuscript. We have been privileged to serve as Hayden's publisher, and we look forward to introducing readers to his poetry for decades to come.

MICHAEL WIEGERS

A poem is not an expression, nor is it an object. Yet it somewhat partakes of both. What a poem is

Is never to be known, for which I have learned to be grateful. But the aspect in which I see my own

Is as the act of love...

—Hayden Carruth, *from* "The Impossible Indispensability of the Ars Poetica"

DOCTOR JAZZ

BY BROOKS HAXTON

In 1979, when I was about to start graduate school in the poetry program at Syracuse University, my wife, Francie, and I rented the upstairs of a house near campus. A few days after we moved in, we met a white-bearded man of about sixty who carried a small box of books up the driveway, wheezing a little and red in the face. He introduced himself as our new downstairs neighbor, Hayden Carruth; and he told me, catching my look of concern, that his doctor warned him he might die soon from a heart attack. I could see that my wife, a nurse, found this easy to believe. After I helped him unload boxes from his car, we invited him upstairs for an impromptu spaghetti dinner and housewarming.

Hayden and I made conversation about Vermont, where he had been living for almost twenty years with his wife and son. I asked him about the wildlife there, because, in his recent poem "Essay," he was so eloquent in his outrage about animals being driven toward extinction:

> They are going away—their fur and their wild eyes,
> their voices. Deer leap and leap in front
> of the screaming snowmobiles until they leap

out of existence. Hawks circle once or twice

above their shattered nests and then they climb

to the stars. I have lived with them fifty years,

we have lived with them fifty million years,

and now they are going, almost gone. I don't know

if the animals are capable of reproach.

But clearly they do not bother to say good-bye.

Gardening came up, as well. Hayden had been raising a good deal of what they ate. When he saw that Francie baked fresh bread, he told us that he used to bake bread for his family, too. Francie and I liked him. I was glad we happened to be neighbors, and I hoped we would be friends.

He had taken a full-time teaching appointment, he said, because his son's graduation from high school and his own divorce had made that practical. He believed, after a recent experience as an adjunct professor in Vermont, that he could handle his agoraphobia well enough, with medication, to be a regular professor. Although his was not the kind of honorary chair that pays inordinately well, a professor's salary was more money, by far, than he had ever made before.

His poetry workshop, which met in a windowless corner room of Bird Library, included four students: a lesbian feminist lawyer who kept her background to herself; a kid from Watts who wrote poems about gang life; and two small-town white boys—me, from the Mississippi Delta, and, from western New York, Dan Moriarty, the student Hayden used to tell me had learned the most from him. After working crummy jobs and living poor for seven years, since college, I was grateful but nervous to be coming back to school. But

Hayden was something much worse than nervous. He had difficulty looking up from the table to face us, his hands trembled badly; we worried that his job might not work out.

But he had a methodical approach to teaching which, he said, had come from writing hundreds of book reviews. He met each poem on its own terms, while describing his experience as a reader in scrupulous detail. Sometimes his critical thinking would veer into a diatribe, against poetry workshops, for example, or against fashions in the literary world. He would curse the lack of passionate feeling in recent poetry, the lack of intellectual seriousness and of technical verve. He did not make unkind remarks about any of us, but he was forthright about where poems had gone wrong. His strength of conviction made us feel free to be candid with one another, but we found it more helpful, most of the time, to listen.

Hayden's fund of knowledge made it no surprise to hear that, as a boy, he had read the *Encyclopædia Britannica*, for pleasure, from A to zed. As a teacher, he spoke in well-turned paragraphs, taking palpable delight in the surprising texture and precision of deliberate word choice.

For the first reading that he gave in Syracuse, he sat in an overstuffed chair with a floor lamp beside it and books and papers on a little table, an imitation of the set for the host of *Masterpiece Theatre*. Every previous reader had stood at the podium, but this was just for Hayden. It conveyed personal immediacy and relieved his anxiety about standing in front of an audience. It also minimized the distraction of holding a text with trembling hands. He had given up his hope of working as a jazz clarinetist largely because of stage fright, and poetry readings had only just begun to seem possible for him. He spent years, after an eighteen-month-long psychiatric hospitalization in his thirties, trying to master the challenge of walking around the block from his parents' house without screaming in the flood of panic. Now, the audience at his reading shared a sense of gratitude for his presence in the program, for his work of the past thirty years, and for the imaginative passion he communicated when he read aloud.

Hayden soon became my mentor. Besides workshops, I took every graduate seminar he taught, on the poetry of Alexander Pope, on the writings of Villon, Wordsworth, Camus, and Goodman, on the history of critical theory, ancient and modern, and on prosody.

That first semester, when the two of us walked home from campus a few times together, I saw that my eagerness made Hayden nervous. But we had so many interests in common, it was difficult for me to accept, at first, that he was being generous to the point of accepting imposition. He did this with dozens of young writers and others eager for his help. Chores born of his generosity dogged him all his life.

That first year the graduate students closest to him were Andy Robbins and Joe-Anne McLaughlin, a couple then, who have gone on, in their separate lives, to write and publish well, though neither has received the attention that their poetry deserves. In those days, as before and later, the faculty and students at Syracuse were close-knit. Besides getting together at readings, receptions, and parties, we enjoyed a small-stakes poker game from time to time, which Hayden, Toby Wolff, and Ray Carver sometimes joined.

Hayden was just finishing ten years' work on *The Sleeping Beauty*, a series of 125 rhymed poems in the variable fifteen-line form he called a paragraph. He returned from his summer in Montana in 1980 with the finished manuscript in hand and invited students to hear him read from it. I was out of town for this, and when I saw him I asked if I might borrow a copy of the poem. What he lent me, in a cardboard box, on heavy cotton paper, was the original, typed on his old manual, without a single correction or typo. When I held the pages of the typescript at home, though I'd grown up among writers, I felt the way one feels in a museum or rare-book room, handling a famous manuscript.

The book as a whole is overwhelmingly powerful, as in the autobiographical vein of paragraphs 66 and 67, a single sentence, which I quote without the numbering, below. The Hatch, in this passage, is one in a series of about thirty topics beginning with the letter *h*, each the focus of a memory or dream. The list includes the names of poets, philosophers, leaders of states and armies, divinities, places, and so on. Homer is the first, and the last appears, with retrospective logic, in the last of the poem's 1,860 lines: "My name is Hayden and I have made this song."

He remembers:
There was this big house they called the Hatch,
Or sometimes the Laughing Academy, which had
barred grilles
On its windows, for every door a latch
And an appropriate lock called Yale
That was big and brassy with a key in someone else's
possession,
And inside there he suffered interrogation, torture
When they wired his head to voltage and shocked him
Deep into the abyss, so that when he woke
He couldn't remember who he had been, and they did it

Again and again, and he sighed,
"Why? What have I done?" and usually they evaded
The question, but sometimes they said,
"Nothing, son, nothing at all—you're just unlucky,"
And he stood by the window in a dirty draft of cold,
Looking out, and he saw benches and sidewalks

Rise up and proclaim themselves, and his skin
Crawled on his body, a tear strolled down his nose,
And months later they said again,
"You're jinxed, son, you'll always
Be this way," and he saw his life sink down
In a melted gray heaving mass like a broken brain,
The chairs ignored him, the calendar
On the wall masturbated shamelessly, relentlessly,
Until years later they said, "O.K., you can go now,
Everything has been done,"
And he stepped to the door, but then he did not know how,
And he turned as if he had lost someone,
And they threw him out, and "Why?" he still
     whispered, "Why?"
Knowing no answer would come to him under the sun
Or anywhere else, whether he should live or die.

Before reading this poem, I had read most of Hayden's
published verse, his two novels, and a number of his essays, but I
had hardly begun to articulate my response. Mastery of rhyme and
meter, conspicuous breadth of lexicon, syntactic deftness, range of
idiom, and improvisational freedom, part jazz, part free verse, had

been hallmarks of Hayden's developing style for years. The voices of naturalist, bard, historian, social critic, philosopher, farmer, mythographer, raconteur, soldier, jazzer, and private person, in love and in pain, all these threads were already strong in the fabric.

Inversions, archaisms, rhetorical flourishes, technical locutions, and a studied complexity of syntax in the construction of thought and feeling are features of the style that one critic called "conventional." This dismissiveness strikes me as the opposite of a useful observation. After all, the *reader* who rejects a style for venturing outside his own milieu is "conventional" in this derogatory sense, while the writer who defies ambient conventionality by ranging among idioms and by using an inheritance from the literary past is *resourceful.* Old-fogeydom is *not* resourcefulness, of course, and resourcefulness is not always a success, nor is it every writer's calling; but stylistic synthesis, informed by current idiom and by history, including archaism, is crucial in a number of writers of the first rank, such as Spenser, Melville, Pound, and Carruth.

After his service in the Army Air Corps in Italy during the last of World War II, Hayden had begun to write poems in a great variety of forms, genres, and styles. At almost forty, long an accomplished writer with serious artistic and intellectual ambitions, he published his first collection. His books chart his development over the next twenty years, from a late, sometimes stilted, sometimes dazzling start, toward an expressive intensity that characterizes the work more and more steadily. By 1978, *Brothers, I Loved You All* represents a sustained artistic consummation that places him, in the words of James Wright, among the "finest poets... at work in the United States." The first poem of this collection gives a kind of *ars poetica,* in the stages of its response to the cry of a loon:

...his song, truly

a vestige, the laugh that transcends

first all mirth

and then all sorrow

and finally all knowledge, dying

into the gentlest quavering timeless

woe.

The jazz session described in the concluding three sections of "Paragraphs" ends the collection with one of literature's most powerful descriptions of jazz, or of any music, a distinction shared, in my view, with "Sonny's Blues" by Baldwin and with passages in Mann's *Doctor Faustus* and in Proust. Poem after poem in the book is indelible.

If Hayden had already entered the company of great American poets, which he had, *The Sleeping Beauty*, nevertheless, worked on a larger scale, demanding to be read as his magnum opus. After it was published a number of poets and critics would find, as I did when I read his pristine typescript, that the work makes good on this aim.

I left Syracuse the following year, and I saw Hayden only a few times over the next decade. His poetry took several distinct turns. He published a collection, *If You Call This Cry a Song*, that followed up on the accomplishment in *Brothers, I Loved You All* and *The Sleeping Beauty* with poems largely about the rural world he knew in Vermont.

His next book was in rhymed, highly enjambed syllabic lines, which were new to him, and in a fresh poetic voice. This was the collection his old friend, publisher and poet James Laughlin, called *Asphalt Georgics.* The poems move through the urban sprawl around Syracuse, speaking in edgier tones to fit the world they inhabit. If

the poems are not as strong as what preceded them, they are still
engaging, especially for their expressive directness and for the refusal
to settle into a proven milieu or method.

Tell Me Again How the White Heron Rises and Flies Across the Nacreous
River at Twilight Toward the Distant Islands takes an equally distinctive tack,
announced with typical lack of restraint in its title. After the counted
syllables and tight rhyming lines of earlier books, these lines sprawl
across the page in rhythms and syntax like those of conversation
or prose. Sometimes the spirit is bucolic and romantic, as here, in a
poem where lovers walk on the towpath by the Erie Canal:

> . . .a long earthen avenue
> Reaching far and straight ahead of us into the shifting
>   veils that hung everywhere in folds, oaks clinging to
>   their dry leaves,
> Bare maples in many shades of gray, the field of
>   goldenrod gone to seed and burnt-out asters,
> Sumac with dark cones, the brown grasses, and at the
>   far edge, away from the canal,
> A line of trees above which towered three white pines in their
>   singular shapes.
> . . . .
> . . .the colors,
> Not forgetting cattails and milkweed, dock and sorbaria, ferns
>   and willows and barberries,
> Were a nearly infinite variety of the soft tones, the subtle
>   tones, made even more indistinct
> In their reflections on the greenish water of the canal. And a
>   light breeze was blowing.

For once I will risk the word *zephyr*, which is right and which
   reminds me of *sapphire*,
And I realize that beneath all these colors lay an undertone of
   blue, the gentle sky as it curls
Below the penumbra of vision. A small yellow butterfly tricked
   its way across the brown field beside us,
And I thought to myself, Where in hell did you come from?
   Last night was a hard frost.
And then I knew it had been born this day, perhaps a moment
   ago, and its life was fluttering, flickering, trickling out in our
   presence...

Sometimes the voice is more satiric, as in the short poem "How
Lewisburg, Pa., Escaped the Avenging Angel":

"Dust," she said. "What is it? Where does it come from?"
"What do you mean dust?" I said.
"Dust," she said. "That stuff that comes back on top of the
   refrigerator three days after you've wiped it off."
"Lint," I said. "Bits of soil. Danders. Carbon. Vegetable matter."
"Oh," she said.
"Generalized metaphysical fall-out," I said. "Dust to dust, etc."
"How do you know?" she said.
"I don't," I said.
"Then kindly refrain from being so fucking authoritative,"
   she said.

As ever, there are meditations on philosophy, history,
poetry, jazz, and country life. In general, the freer line unfolds with

inclusiveness of thought and perception, with the expansiveness of feeling that characterizes Hayden's poetry at its best.

The most powerful poem in the collection is the last, "Mother." In response to the difficult decline and death of Hayden's mother, he uses the same long free-verse line as the rest of this book, but here he ends almost every line with a distinct pause, which contributes to the elegiac pace and building sonorousness. "Mother," in its fusion of abstract thought, event, and emotional expression, is another of the Carruth poems that makes my short list of American masterpieces.

In the winter of 1988, having taken an overdose of pills, Hayden was discovered unconscious and was revived, after his heart stopped, by emergency medical personnel. Fully recovered, he found himself, for some reason, delighted to be alive. He describes this experience with an eerily dispassionate calm in the first essay of his collection *Suicides and Jazzers.* Later that year, on a meandering drive in the country, Hayden happened to see a small ramshackle house off Highway 46 a little south of Munnsville, New York. Since it was a few miles from the edge of the earth and in slight disrepair, it was for sale at a price Hayden could afford. Joe-Anne happened to be back in the area, and, after having seen little of one another for some years, they fell in love, married, and settled there.

Hayden soon retired from Syracuse University, and I returned to teach in 1993, again finding a house near campus. Straight off I started visiting Munnsville. A few times, I drove out with friends, or sometimes other friends of theirs or family would be visiting when I came. For Hayden's birthdays they would throw big picnics. But, mostly, it would be just we three, Hayden, Joe-Anne, and I. We walked in the spring woods when the trilliums came up. We consulted the field guides about local flowers. When it got warmer, we watched the hawks ride thermals over the wall of the quarry, where they nested. I stayed once in a blizzard, and they were amused at my wide-eyed Southerner's take on a four-foot snowfall. For most of my visits, any time of year, we sat at the kitchen table by a big window and talked. Chickadees and finches came and went at the birdfeeder. Bluebirds flew back and forth from their nest in the garage. Hayden, Joe-Anne, and I talked about what was happening in the world and worked, against our dire proclivities, at cracking each other up.

From Hayden's late sixties into his seventies, despite his claims to the contrary, he was strong and steady on his feet. And even as his health began to fail, he kept writing well: the new poems in his *Collected Shorter Poems, Scrambled Eggs and Whiskey, Doctor Jazz, Toward the Distant Islands,* and the last poems collected here. He also turned toward more personal topics in his prose, publishing a collection of autobiographical essays he called *Reluctantly;* a book of reminiscence about James Laughlin, the founder of New Directions and a bafflingly undervalued poet; and a book of letters that he wrote to his friend Jane Kenyon during her final illness.

His daughter, Martha, ill for several years with cancer, died in her middle age. Many of Hayden's friends died, too. His health declined. He used a cane. After his fainting spells, he needed vascular surgery, and after a major coronary, heart surgery, which laid him up with life-threatening pneumonia. He spent seven years on oxygen, lost vision in one eye and then the other. All this was more difficult because of his lifelong depression. Finally, in his last few weeks, came a series of strokes, which at first left him uncharacteristically animated and cheerful. He died at eighty-seven, home in bed, in Joe-Anne's arms.

Because he kept writing well, his last poems include, among other things, a vivid and revealing chronicle of old age. Hayden celebrated the delight that poems give by saying what matters, even about devastation. He praised his friend Raymond Carver, in his elegy "Ray," for "those last poems written / after he knew," good poems, "most of them," though Hayden is rueful, a few lines later: "What crazies we writers are, / our heads full of language like buckets of minnows / standing in the moonlight on a dock."

Hayden wrote movingly about psychiatric illness, and the work from his last two decades, haunted by physical decline, includes many first-rate poems. Still, I feel called upon, as I conclude this essay, to point out what must be obvious: his art stands as the achievement of imaginative wholeness, of the passion of deliberative intelligence, which he considered an important affirmation of humanity in the teeth of an indifferent universe. Sometimes, when he went overboard, Hayden groused and foresaw doom until even his fellow grumblers, some of us, laughed, and he would catch himself and laugh along. Doom arrived in his lifetime, in his personal experience and in the wide world, often enough to make the darkness in his disposition sensible, but he was better known among his many friends for warmth and generosity.

In one of his best essays, he praised poetry as the "expression of subjectivity moving through and beyond itself," what he calls, in the phrasing of that essay's title, "The Act of Love." This is the core of moral and imaginative value affirmed in Hayden's work and life, as he says to the forty-one jazz musicians listed by name in one of his paragraphs: "Brothers I loved you all." Now, for us, reading his poems is what it was for him to hear recordings from the masters, art leading us beyond ourselves into the great, good company where we find ourselves again.

HAYDEN CARRUTH

STEPHEN DOBYNS

Hayden Carruth's writing life lasted about seventy years. Stanley Kunitz's lasted longer; Thomas Hardy's matched it. During that time, Hayden wrote formal poems, including a book of sonnets, and free-verse poems, some influenced by Whitman and some written in what are called "experimental forms." He wrote poems with very long lines and poems with very short lines. He wrote haiku and he wrote a collection of poetic faxes. He wrote four-line poems and 500-line poems. He wrote in Latinate syntax and broken syntax. His language could be densely romantic, flatly journalistic, or countrified. He wrote funny poems, political poems, and poems that could make you cry. Yet, despite these differences, each poem was clearly a Hayden Carruth poem. In terms of his craft, he became a great technician. In terms of his content, he could squeeze your heart.

Hayden called himself an anarchist—"People are smart enough to govern themselves without a government"—but he easily became autocratic when talking about poetry or when his opinions were challenged. Still, he had the egalitarianism necessary to an anarchist. His poetry is full of the names of friends, living and dead, yet he was afraid of groups of people, even small groups. He was the sanest man I knew and yet all his life he struggled with sanity, a struggle that included a long visit to a hatch, or loony bin, as he called it, in his late thirties, and three years holed up in his bedroom in his parents' house in Connecticut. He was afraid of walking across the middle of the large quadrangle at Syracuse University for fear of being sucked up into the sky. He was afraid to go to a Syracuse graduation, where he was supposed to get an honorary degree, because of all the people.

Along with Bill Knott, Hayden was one of our very best writers of love poems, which is vaguely ironic, since both men are and were terribly shy. He gave his first reading at fifty-seven; it had been that long a time before he could summon up the nerve.

Hayden came from a family of journalists in Connecticut, and he believed a poet should be able to write everything: journalism, book reviews, essays of all sorts, and fiction. For the many years he lived in Vermont, he supported himself with what he called "hackwork": editorial work and writing book reviews, op-ed articles, and essays. He also put together *the* best anthology of twentieth-century American poetry: *The Voice That Is Great Within Us.* Hayden was a constant letter writer. Students, ex-students, friends, acquaintances, strangers—his letters could fill half a dozen thick volumes. He also read the manuscripts of all his friends—a large and prickly bunch—and of many former students. His suggestions were tactful and smart. A fierce proofreader, he could spot a comma fault faster than one might spot a nearby elephant. He never talked down to anyone. He was incapable of lying, incapable of small-mindedness, incapable of being cruel—unless he'd had too much to drink, which was a reason he stopped drinking for thirty years.

These apparent contradictions continue. He was a great talker and at times he would refuse to talk to anyone for days. He knew machinery and farming but could do nothing in the kitchen. Even making coffee was a struggle. He once visited our house in Boston for two weeks, when I was elsewhere, and my wife, who quickly tired of cooking for him, bought him twelve different frozen dinners. He was completely satisfied.

Beyond poetry and his friends, what he liked best were sex, jazz, and books, but jazz sustained him till the end. He would sit in my living room with his head back on the couch, his eyes shut, and listen to Ben Webster, Sidney Bechet, or a half dozen others. He would grunt or moan at the bits he particularly liked. Even after a favorite song he might have heard five hundred times, he would slap his knee and say, "God, that was great," just as if it were the first time. He seemed to know the name of every musician in every group. One of his life's grand moments was when he saw Billie Holiday in a small club in New York before the war. He described her as one of the world's most beautiful women and kept a poster of her on his wall in Munnsville. He'd said that the piece of music he most wanted to be played at his funeral was Billie Holiday's "Please Don't Talk About Me When I'm Gone."

But as with Philip Larkin, Hayden didn't like jazz from bebop forward. Thelonious Monk meant nothing to him. John Coltrane was a cipher. I realized at one point that what he disliked about modern jazz was its expressionistic and existential aspect; he disliked the solitude and complaining. What he loved were the small groups of the 1930s and '40s. He loved their joy, their sense of community and sharing. Sidney Bechet, Vic Dickenson, Wild Bill Davison—these men had intense, musical conversations with one another instead of dwelling on personal angst. Hayden played the clarinet in a ragged way and at one point had joined into small Dixieland sessions with his friends. He liked how a group of musicians could be like one interesting and complicated person, a benevolent hydra who, by using their combined skills, could make something approaching beauty. As with many poets who are viscerally connected to music, he had a very good ear. Here are the first six lines of the first poem in his *Collected Shorter Poems:* "The Wreck of a Circus Train."

> Couplings buckled, cracked, collapsed,
> And all reared, wheels and steel,
> Pawing and leaping above the plain,
>
> And fell down totally, a crash
> Deep in the rising surf of dust,
> As temples into their cellars crash.

Here are alliteration and a clash of consonants, rhythm and internal rhyme, a breathlessness: if Hayden could have played jazz, this is what he'd have played.

Hayden deeply distrusted the world made by human beings and disliked the messes they had left. As he moved into old age, he became more of a curmudgeon; then, in his last years, he became something of a Luddite and engaged in ferocious diatribes against the Internet and cell phones, M.F.A. programs, contemporary grammar, diction, and music. It was a long list. Had he known about Twitter, he would have become apoplectic.

Deep down, Hayden felt he didn't understand the world, although he had many opinions about it. The world seemed foreign to him; he couldn't understand why people behaved as they did; he couldn't understand cruelty. Either he or the world was in a deep fog, and he hoped it wasn't him. He dealt with these feelings through isolation, alcohol, and music, but mostly he dealt with them through poetry. Poetry became a buffer between him and the world, and it became the tool by which he tried to understand the world. Poetry linked him to the great mass of people he didn't care to meet face-to-face. His constant task was to turn outside reality into language, to freeze the fleeting moment. This was one of the reasons he wrote in so many styles and forms, so many tones and moods, so many kinds of diction. He was trying to get it right, to be exact. But, of course, one can never get it right. The word is always a diminishment of what one tries to describe. Even if each poem is perfect, it still seems not enough. And so one tries again and again, and the poems pile up like used artillery shells. Hayden tried to take the world out of its fog and make it real. He tried to see himself in relation to the world. He tried to make sense of it, first for himself, then for others. This sort of worked. At least poetry kept him alive, because I doubt he could have lived without it. Poetry was his lifeline.

The first times we met were several evenings in the houses of Ray Carver and Toby Wolff in Syracuse. It was the fall semester of 1985 and I was there to teach several classes. Hayden looked like a disheveled farmer. He was grumpy, unfriendly, and wouldn't talk to me. But it was clear that Ray and Toby liked him and deeply respected him, so I kept quiet.

I next met him in the fall of 1987. My wife and I and the children had moved to Syracuse, where I was teaching full-time. I liked to cook, drink, and have groups of people over for dinner, so twice that fall I invited Hayden with Ray and Tess Gallagher, Toby and his wife Catherine, and some others. Both times, Hayden was grumpy and silent the whole evening. It didn't occur to me that he was shy and unhappy in his relationship with his girlfriend. In my egocentric way, I'd assumed his behavior meant he didn't like me. Later that fall, Hayden's girlfriend left him and then he took every pill in the house. He was in a coma in the hospital in Utica for five days. The doctor never thought he would live.

The day after Hayden regained consciousness, my wife gathered up our two girls—three and seven—and went to visit him. I was astounded; she hardly knew him, had hardly talked to him. But she's Chilean and believes that even if you hardly know a person, you go to the hospital to encourage them and let them know you care about them. Hayden, too, was astounded.

Because Hayden had tried to commit suicide, he was soon sent to the Benjamin Rush psychiatric center in Syracuse. It was a dreary place, full of cigarette smoke and sad teenage anorexics with bandages where they had cut themselves. We saw him twice and then adopted him, as it were. We had him signed over to our care. It was like freeing a puppy from the pound, and his mood changed entirely. He stayed at our house for three weeks and then for two more when he had a little setback. During that time we became close friends, and for the next seven years that we remained in Syracuse, he came to our house once or twice a week. Sometimes my wife and I would visit him in his small, book-stuffed house in Munnsville, about forty miles away. At my house, we would have dinner and drink, talk, and listen to music until the early morning. Then he would stay over. His new wife, Joe-Anne McLaughlin-Carruth, came with him. Mostly we didn't get drunk, but we became fairly sodden, though this got worse as the years passed. He treated my children as small adults and spent time with my wife in her garden. He knew the names of all the plants and birds. Although I had listened to jazz all my life, I learned much more about it from him. The fact of his death particularly struck me when, a few days after, I had a question about jazz and realized I had no one to ask.

He was an extremely heavy smoker, and the walls and ceilings of his small house were yellow with old smoke. The spines of the books were covered with it; they looked like a single set of yellow-bound books. Being there was like being inside an ashtray. Then he quit abruptly and completely, after a heart attack, when he was eighty-two.

When he'd had the heart attack, he was taken to a Utica hospital. At around 2 a.m., a nurse found him wandering the halls, smoking one cigarette after another, dragging his oxygen tank behind him. He and the nurse had a few pointed words, and then she threatened to call the police. He never smoked after that. Just after he turned eighty-seven, though, he had a small stroke and passed out. When he came to, he had forgotten he no longer smoked and demanded a cigarette from Joe-Anne. He became quite rude about it. Talking to me on the phone, he denied that he had quit. "It's crazy to think I'd ever quit smoking," he said. It took a week to convince him.

Hayden, as might be supposed, was somewhat eccentric, and the people who knew him have lots of stories, but he was kind and generous, and he had a great deep laugh that would bring tears to his eyes. I would tell jokes just to hear that laugh. He was also a brilliant and wonderful poet who saw himself as still learning his craft, still growing, but he never talked about his poetry unless questioned and prodded. After my wife and I left Syracuse in 1995, we obviously saw less of him, but we visited, talked on the phone, and wrote letters—

he much more than I—but it was like eating the menu instead of the meal. It didn't satisfy.

I would ask him on the phone what he was writing and he would say, "Oh no, I'm not writing anymore, just some scribbling." All he did, he said, was play computer solitaire, read mystery novels, and watch basketball on TV. I asked him the same question regularly over the next twelve years, and his answer hardly changed. "My brain is gone," he'd say. "I can't concentrate. I'm finished." But in fact he wrote nearly every day. He put together a collection of autobiographical essays. He published *Letters to Jane*, the letters to the poet Jane Kenyon that he had written daily over the last year of her life. He wrote essays. He wrote a short book about his friend James Laughlin. He wrote several hundred letters. He read people's manuscripts. He finished the poems that went into *Scrambled Eggs and Whiskey*, which won the National Book Award; he wrote the poems that went into the long *Doctor Jazz*, published in 2003; he wrote the new poem section of *Toward the Distant Islands: New and Selected Poems*, published in 2006; and he wrote the collection of poems that you must be holding in your hands.

In fact, it was impossible for him not to write. As I said, it was how he dealt with the world, how he came to terms with it, how he could admit his love for it, embracing it and keeping it at arm's length at the same time. As he wrote in "Poem No. X": "What can an old poet do at the end of time / But scratch out nightmare verses in the old / Remembered measures that have endured / For centuries before him?" Some of the new poems in this book are fragments, some are occasional poems, and some are among his best. As might be expected, many deal with aging and imminent death. However, since 1985 I regularly heard him say that he expected to die before the year was out. Telling me and everyone else was like a nervous tic. He would claim that he had strange pains; his heart was acting up. But his heart attack at eighty-two was his first; the doctor said he'd had the heart of a horse.

In contrast, during the last fifteen years of his life he often told me that the past twenty years had been his best and happiest. It was hard for him to trust happiness until it had passed, or so he thought, but then he would enjoy it in memory and freeze it in time by writing about it.

One night in September 2008, Joe-Anne called me when my wife and I were driving to New Hampshire. She said Hayden was in a hospital in Utica and dying. He'd had several strokes. I turned the car in that direction. When we saw Hayden later that night, he was either unconscious or asleep, though he made a noise when my wife touched his cheek and said his name. He looked somewhat like Walt Whitman in his last days. About a dozen years before, a Syracuse barber had done a bad job trimming his beard, making it lopsided, and Hayden swore never to trim his beard again. Then he stopped having haircuts, nor would he trim his eyebrows. There was a large white mitt on each hand; they were supposed to keep him from pulling out his catheter, which he kept groping for. He was blind in one eye from a botched cataract operation a year or so before. The guilty doctor had wept and Hayden had comforted her, telling her he forgave her. The other eye was three-fourths gone. Despite this, he was still handsome and had most of his hair, and his wrinkles seemed to be fading away.

The next morning, when we returned to the hospital, he was still unconscious, though he muttered a little. Joe-Anne said we should read poems to him. Brooks Haxton read some of Hayden's own poems and I read him Shakespeare sonnets. As Hayden lay in his hospital bed, he seemed to be approaching his end, but in fact he was returning to consciousness. The next day he could talk a little, in a slurred sort of way, and he laughed his deep laugh when Joe-Anne read him a funny letter from a friend. He seemed fairly clearheaded, but at the bottom of a deep well. I couldn't think of anything to say except to tell him I loved him, but my wife was able to talk to him and could understand what he said in reply.

The next day I had to leave. My wife stayed and went with Hayden when he was taken back to his house in Munnsville. For several days, she helped Joe-Anne take care of him. Then he died, and it was hard not to hear Hamlet's last words: "The rest is silence." There comes a point, when a person is dying, that you realize dying is the best thing he or she can do. But what a trail of events is strung out behind each of us, like the tails of comets.

I was uncertain about writing this essay; it seemed I knew too much and knew too little. I was afraid of exaggerating him or diminishing him. I didn't understand how I could keep it under a hundred pages. But his life is in his poems for all to see. As I was writing, my youngest child called from Philadelphia. She is twenty-five. She asked what I was doing, and I told her. She said, "It must be wonderful to write about him. It must be like spending time with your friend again."

I had not thought of it like that, but she was correct. The moment happens, is tasted, and is gone.

Father's Day

Well. Sylphie, it's another shitty morning
In Upstate New York, as usual. A gray sky
Lies on the treetops, and the air is cold
And damp. I don't know what fathers are
Supposed to do, although the calendar says
This is "Father's Day." But the day is gloomy
And not at all conducive to visiting or
Celebrating. I know the best thing fathers in
Their prime can do is to make daughters and
More daughters; we can never have enough.
Daughters are our best protection against
Loneliness and the absurd atrocities of
Foreign policy. And in fact some years ago
I did my part in this endeavor. Yes, I did.
I sired and raised a most delightful daughter,
Beautiful and intelligent and artistically gifted.
But then, through no fault of mine or hers,
Our endeavor failed most miserably, and now
You are my only daughter, Sylphie, in your
Splendid adolescence. You share my days
And often my nights too. Your love teases
Me and your wisdom comforts me. My dear,
Some people say that you are "only a cat,"
But you are a daughter to me, my solace and
My joy. Truly you are. Oh, Sylphie, stay
With me as long as I am here. It won't be
Very long, dear girl, but I need you for a while.

H.C., June 12, 2006

XLIII

LAST POEMS FROM PREVIOUSLY
PUBLISHED WORKS

The Birth of Venus

Surely we knew our darkling shore.
None doubted that continual roar
Of gray waves seething, cold and huge,
None misconceived that beach, those reeds
Wreathed in the dark, dead, dripping weeds.
No fiction there, no subterfuge.

Came she then, borne from such sea-bed?
We think so. Clouds in violent red
Shone on her warmly, flank and breast,
And some remember how the foam
Swirled at her ankles. Other some
Look shrewd and smile behind the rest.

She gave us beauty where our eyes
Had seen need only. We grew wise,
For how could wisdom fail the gift
Bestowed in that superb undress,
Value devised as loveliness
From ocean's riches, ocean's thrift?

But, Love, then must it be the sea
That makes you credible? Must we
Bear all to one phenomenon?
True, certainty is our seacoast,
The landmark of the clearly lost
Whose gathering waves drive on and on.

Great queen, an ignorant poet's heart
Is all his faith, yet still his art
Can prick your source to tell the truth.
So teach him, lady. Then always
Among the people here who praise
Your powers, one will be Carruth.

Journey to a Known Place (1961)

IV. Ignis

Upward into the dome of brilliance, limping:
I, the tired climber, acquiring strength
From fatigue, weakness repaired in desire;
I, mounting, going where the stout clumps
Of wild wheat purply ripened, among rocks
Glowing like porcelain now, like jade, among
Silken grasses flowing in flame-like waves,
Among the increasing flowers, thickening trees,
The purslane bedded between the roots of oak,
Aspiring now in sun's cascading element,
Splendors upbranching, the palpitant leafing blood.

    Sing, little voice,
    Of the sun, lordly
    And lovely, eloquent
    Boy of the light
    So meaning, so dumb
    That at last it is
    This one, the small one,
    Our princeling who levels us,
    Marries us, tumbles us,
    Scarred or untouched,
    In the crowded garden.
    Sing, little voice,
    The imperfect song
    Of done and done,
    Imperfect and wrong:

Right with the sun,

Our infant, lordly

And lovely, leveling

All. For the light

Alone does pierce

Armor and shell

And the knurling skull,

Giving done and done,

One and one,

To behold: each

In each. Inward

The light enters

Each darkness alike,

And in similitude

Is understanding.

Sing, little voice,

The imperfect song

Of gratefulness

As my shadow,

Handsomer, sings.

"Light, which moves at the rate of 186,000 miles
Per second, requires 100,000 years to cross
From one rim of our galaxy to the other rim."
Tell me, I murmured, tell me what does it mean
At this way station? For God's sake, interpret
Me this, I mumbled. "The light-sensitive elements
Of the human retina number 1,000 billions..."
Nailed to the raft of sense, swept by the magnitudes.

Upward into the dome of brilliance, limping:
And the gemlike rock glowed under the mosses,
And ferns splayed like cool flames, and trees
Lifted, arching and strained to the august sky;
And there were open places where I found
Other journeyers, resting or climbing, strangers,
Sweet eyes once cracked in the torturing cold;
And some few I saw known to me, and one was
A woman I had once married, now like a soft ash
Inly aglow, rippling the violet of mind's smile
Like the concentricities of a woodland pool.
And our hands' touching sang the small cockcrow
As for night's ending, across the distant fields.
So through the alert forests we advanced
Together, by streams that leapt faultlessly
To the far nether sea, crystalline, syllabled,
By savor's herbs, spilt flowers on the way,
The vines and berry trees bright with their meat,
Each blossom in separate need conjointly gendered,
Simple and brave, shaped by a seasonal sap
To the forms of earth in its sovereign histories;
And so we two, there in a private place
Of hot endeavor, as root and bud and bloom,
The bronze sky ringing above, the wild wheat singing.

Proven never,
Being riven
By a steely word
That seals and deafens,

Till, until
One is but one
And all affrighted,
Lone, alone—
Still no treason,
Time or distance,
Quells the quick
Supposing faith;
Will and reason
Drive the breath:
You, you, you.

And I had seen the scarred small breast
Of the hurt woman, imperfect, wounded, wakening
In my body the honeyed and flowing anguish
Of her being weighed on my lameness; but it
Was love. And afterward we went on,
Climbing together into the fire, the flames
Seeming to touch us, flittering on our arms,
Purifying us, so that the shimmer and gleam
Moved between us as the force of our desire,
Altering in our humility beyond desire
To acceptance, each of himself in the other truly;
And of these still other ones, these multitudes
Converging now as the mount narrowed,
Moving upward together in need as food of
The earth, up in the heat of the marrying sun.

Light is the force that alone resists the wind,
Stays, unwavering, though the wind sweeps by.

And often our hands reached out in guidance
Or assistance, for scarcely a one was unwounded
And eyes I saw ill placed in the mask of shock.
Yes, tongues had been torn out, backs
Had been furrowed with lashes, many an eye
Blinded, many a limb broken, and the
Able of body walked with a shackling gait.
In truth this journey was the painfullest,
Gravest; and in this we knew one another,
Losing for a rare time the futility of words.

    To stake it all,
    The need and the response,
    The point from which
    Intelligence went forth,
    The failing quality
    Of aspiration
    In which one found
    One's strength, the walled
    Terrors in which one
    Found love, and finally
    The indifferent space
    Everywhere dividing
    Individual worth,
    To stake it all
    On a flawed, soft,
    Abused and unreliable,
    Imperfect word:
    Magnanimity.

And up, far, far, the astral banks, and then?
Nowhereness broods there? Contemplates this hatch?
Dictum, denial: either way absurd.
And that's the horror, that too in part of the song.

To the last woodland ridge, to the summit we came,
Where the forest parted, withdrew from the broadening road,
And where in the humming sun the journeyers gathered,
Groups walking easily now, the highways converging;
And when with a murmur and extending of arms we came
To the place where the city of gold lay visible,
We paused briefly to marvel, and passed on to the
Avenues continuing among scenes of consummate
Splendor, arches and arabesque all agleam in the
Sun, the golden and emerald tiles, and the folk there,
Both the fair-born ones of the city and those others,
Our immigrant people, greeting us as we moved
On wondering feet onward, still toward the center.
And we came at last to the park where the city opened
Round an emblazoned zone and the light, liquescent
And shimmering, seemed a golden-roseate intensity,
Seemed as a fountain ascending, whose returning flow
Made the sunfire's cascade, swirling and vaporing.
And in the midst was the great wheel rising, turning
In music and light, where the people rode in their
Separateness all together, ascending and equally
Descending in the light, instructed at each place
Of the wheel's endlessness. And there the multitude

Assembled, crowding in the unity of concord, all
Estates and relations of being but chiefly the
Female and the male together, joined in desire's
Known imperfectibilities, the great loves with the less,
Always unequal, able and unable making
Each of his opposite anguish the cause of love,
And this was a real urbanity. Holiday, holiday,
The sun and the wheel, and my companion and I
Hand in hand by the edge of the park; until
We also stepped forward, identities, we with the
Others, the gimp and the aging lady, two notes
Of the flute. And for once unambiguously
All was turned to account; and I saw how the
Bitter bitter shame, terror, quick retaliation
And lust, yes, even ignorance that is called evil,
The enormous relative compassment complete,
The rebellion too, the heart's grand assertions
Against the ruins of broken works and days,
All fact, all dream—how from this we make,
Each in his only ascertainable center,
The world of realization, the suffered reality,
Through which comes understanding; or, if not
Understanding, at least the person fleshed
Sufficiently, sufficiently in love's fragments
That gleam in the rubbish of cruelty and wrong:
To know what it is to receive what one has given,
As in a kiss, to bear and to be born,
To see the earth beneath the heron's eye.

Anything ends
In its beginning,
The circles turning
Slowly, so slowly,
Quern of the beat
Of the downrunning heart.
The sunlight fell like diamonds
But did not slacken
Remembrance's forewarning
Of cold and dark to come,
The journey retaken
Without end,
Without end.

And so purity was compounded of impurity.
My spirit rose, a leaf above the fire.
In poverty of means was the authentic end.
Ah, the rack's song. Who shall turn the wheel?
Who shall give up his bones to be parted?
Our guilt contorts the images of our mercy,
But is not our humility more than we thought,
More than a last refuge of the aggressive mind?
And in our knowing, even unto all unknowing,
We are, we are, spite of a foolish end
Under your ancient brightness, O grave stars!
From this we speak and our speech is love,

      Without witness, simply and for the day.

The Norfolk Poems (1962)

R.M.D.

There's rosemary, that's for remembrance...

Somewhere in the hour
Or two or three
While I was by this flower
Meaning constancy
Seven winds cried in a tower
Hollowly.

North Winter (1964)

Afterword:
What the Poet Had Written

...and sun the blear sun straggled forever
     on the horizon an unvarying scrutiny around
around as they limped and stumbled holding
     each other against the wind over the ice
that crumbled under them in the tremors of
     unseen currents and the compass plunging
and rearing the sun the livid sun smeared
     in the wind watching watching never
relenting till exhaustion inundated them
     yet they slept with their eyes open clinging
together just as they walked often with
     their eyes shut hand in hand and fell
at last tripped on their destination
     their sextant snagged their compass wild
with incomprehension and they looked
     over the sides of the world   The sun
the bloated sun ever on the horizon ballooning
     and they shuddered and turned to each other
and then dropped down their plumbline
     under them and payed out its knots
hand over hand to the end to fifteen hundred
     fathoms and felt the plummet still swinging in
the void...

        ...nothing they were nothing
    afloat on nothing frozen by the winds of
nothing under the meaningless glare of nothing's
    eye there where the compass points down
there where the needle turns in...

                                    ...why
    had they come so far what had led them
drawn them into the remoteness and the
    hostility of north what did north mean
and why why was one of them black and
    the other white these were the points in
doubt   There in confrontation they gave over
    the last dissemblings and the last nostalgias
nothing against nothing yet more than that
    their infinitesimal nothing against the
nothing of all the nothing of the real and in
    this giddiness they became at last
the objectivists   They drew back not in
    fear for fear had consumed itself
but as the painter retreats from his canvas
    and so they saved themselves now seeing
how this was the only virtue the withdrawing
    mind that steadies before reality and they
turned slowly together through the whole
    arc of absurdity with outstretched hands
bestowing cold benediction on the north
    and then sank down   Another confrontation

murdered them as they peered in each other's
    eyes...

        ...and saw nothing nothing   Oh
in the low guttural inner voice they proclaimed
    the misery and destitution of nothing...

...and saw nothing except yes this is the
    object nothing except the other's returning
gaze which each knew also saw

              nothing

               And
    in this likeness this scrap of likeness that
contained their likelihood they arose once
    more calmly the tall twin centers
of compassion in the wide field of cold and
    horror   And the sun the huge sun circled
around them...

        ...they came back trudging
    in love and hardship while the sun
took a month to set cowering lidless on the
    extremity of the ice floe where they
crouched   Aurora flickered and mounted
    pale brightening caparisons of yellow
and green falling fluttering swaying
    in such majestic movements that that
elemental silence pealed with trumpets

and they truly listened with their eyes   Did
they then see with their ears the changing
    counterpoints of wind and snow the
purity of whiteness modulating everywhere
    in dunes and fastnesses and cascades
Reality gladdened them and all the more
    when the astonished walrus fell off his seat
backwards whopping the sea and they smote
    their knees and wallowed in the snow...

...north is a horror from which a horror grows
    a purity and fervor to which in opposition
an equal purity and fervor supervene north
    is the latitude of the near remote lying
beyond hope and beyond despair lying in destination
    where the compass points down the needle turns in
where the last breath of meaning is borne away
    on the cold wind north is the meaninglessness
of beauty uncaused in the complete object
    auroral flickerings on the eternal snows
the eye swimming in the mind's deluge
    the blue mountain floating on emptiness
the shadow of the white bear gliding underfoot
    north is the vacancy that flowers in a
glance wakening compassion and mercy and
    lovingkindness the beautiful dew
of the sea rosmarine the call crying in silence
    so distant so small and meeting
itself in its own silence forever north is

north is the aurora north is
deliverance emancipation...

                                        ... north is

nothing...

Nothing for Tigers (1965)

Michigan Water: A Few Riffs Before Dawn

(in memory of Richard Wright)

I

This hour is best, darkening
in absences; loud lights quieten
in a room in a city in the West.

Hour of calm, hour of silences,
silence lingering between the beats;
hour of distances, hour of sadnesses.

Listen, the softly thinking drum
measures the silence in which the bass
murmurs to make the meaning come.

Tranquilly my fingers contemplate
the bone they are, the bone they meet—
these keys breathing among shadows.

Silence holds the sweetness in the tune.
But now who cares? Will our affection,
the great slow sound, tell anything?

Visionaries sauntering in the sound,
you ten well-drunken in dark and light,
sing well, define, dream down the land.

What in the hour, and what in the heart
of sadness, sings in the song's shadow?
Sweet silence, is it then Chicago?

2

Define. So the drum commands,
so the bass entreats. Define.
Ten black men setting out to dine.

Food of heaven had they none,
food of hell was so damned sweet
they sought and sought, and they had none.

The rope, the knife, the stone, the gun,
the train, the door, the cave, the tree,
the sign, the shutter, the snow, the dead.

Impossible to see, impossible!—
in the lake a wheel turning,
in the water a flaming wheel turning.

Like drowned rats, sodden in the dawn,
back through the streets they bring him
in dead march, the watery one.

Dawn comes to the city as to a cellar,
always gray, seeping, always gray,
and we call it, naturally, Pain of Day.

At one rotten moment of the light
the room stops, neither day nor night,
the music falters, neither black nor white.

3

My brother and I, without hope,
set forth upon the city, going
in a white cart drawn by a black goat.

The goat was singing as he must,
my brother and I were not so brave.
The sun hove, shaken in his lust.

We stopped now here, now there
at rusty doors to take upon us
Godspeed and the departing cheers.

They gave us gifts of huge sums
of money. One gave his old coat.
Another gave his old fat wife.

"Good-bye, good-bye..." We went on.
We were hungry. Near the airport
in a field we killed and ate the goat.

Nothing whatever happened, except
my brother who had been weeping smiled
and I who had been smiling wept.

Hence, scorched in that field, we knew
we were successful. When we returned
indeed the people gave us angry faces.

4

Listen, in night's last tender hour,
listen, the somewhat stronger beating—
Chicago, our only city, speaking.

Steel: Shall I not, my children,
grow ever brighter, stiffening
against you my abominable beauty?

Concrete: Ah, I crumble! Back
to earth, sterile, changed,
a hundred lives at every crack!

Glass: Thought you would build a
museum case to house you? True enough,
I'll gleam forever. Wait and see.

Chrome: Even I, in my tarnish,
will stay forever in my opposition
to you: I can never diminish.

Brick: Your fathers knew something of touch
and skill and excellence in shaping,
something of gratitude; but not much.

All: Wind, water, stars, and all things
hard and mindless are our company.
Make your music; the night was long.

5

My Chicago, city of all
the world, strewn
humble-jumble on a wild lakeshore.

We had at one time a beast,
a gorilla, famous among men,
and we kept it at the Lincoln Park Zoo.

In the heart of the city we had a beast
famous among men for power,
natural beauty, pride, and malevolence.

Its eyes bloomed like unlucky flowers
in a rock-cleft face, nodding in the wind
of emptiness nowhere beyond the cage.

The beast died prematurely of a heart
attack; which is to say, of fear.
And it was mourned almost everywhere.

The sun will shine in my back door
some day. But Lord the beast is taken,
taken Lord, taken and taken away.

Listen, the lake waters are seeping
in a thousand conduits, creeping
under the pavement. Listen.

6

In the cage no word is spoken,
no power of darkness
covers the eyes with forgetting.

In the cage no amnesty
waits in the government of the days,
no behoof, no behest.

In the cage no listener hears
these superb particular concussions
of blood, neither a brother nor a sister.

In the cage the moon is irrelevant,
the sun unintelligible,
and the constellations unrecognizable.

In the cage laughter is courage
and courage is laughter and laughter
is courage is laughter is——*the cage!*

In the cage knowledge is the cage
and the comfort of knowledge
is an exceedingly narrow comfort.

Days succeed and fail. What more?
Nothing, except the murmured "no"
after the clanging of the door.

7

Gray dawn seeping through stone—
see, the room blanches. Let the beat
intensify. Between bone and bone

the little blood aches with rain
and the tones deepen. Music!
Given all to Saint Harmony, all,

the pain, the awareness of the pain.
That is all. Music is heard
in one heart, harmony's great chord

in one conscience only; and yet
there is this not explained reaching,
touching, extending, as if the pain

could gather each of us to its own
being. Is it possible? The drum
murmurs against the graylight dawn,

the bass, in unison now, is calm,
the piano descends firmly. Chicago,
city of our music, the long "no,"

listen; the night was a good song;

and we are a true city, rising

in the unjust hour, honorable and strong.

Contra Mortem (1967)

The Wheel of Being II

Such figures if they succeed are beautiful

because for a moment we brighten in a blaze of rhymes

and yet they always fail and must fail

and give way to other poems

in the endless approximations of what we feel

Hopeless it is hopeless   Only the wheel

endures   It spins and spins winding

the was the is the willbe out of nothing

and thus we are   Thus on the wheel we touch

each to each a part

of the great determining reality   How much

we give to one another   Perhaps our art

succeeds after all our small song done in the faith

of lovers who endlessly change heart for heart

as the gift of being   Come let us sing against death.

My Father's Face

Old he was but not yet wax,
old and old but not yet gray.
What an awkwardness of facts
gray and waxen when he lay.

Rage had held me forty years,
only five have sought his grace.
Will my disproportionate tears
quell at last his smiling face?

Awkwardly at his behest
I this queer rhyme try to make
after one that he loved best,
made long since by Willy Blake.

***

Cannot. In
my own way, half inarticulate,
must sing the blues.

Oh how he lay there
quiet as cast dice, crooked. They had given him
a face he never wore

smiling like anyone,
like God—
he, my own, who had smiled only

in the smear of pain,
as now my hemlock smears in this wind
dripping with half-snow, half-rain.

Smoke flares from my stovepipe,
breaks sharply down, away,
blue, whipping the leafless alders, vanishing,

while I watch from my window, this shack
in a scrap of meadow
going to woods—

alder, chokecherry, yellow birch, ash,
and the one old hemlock leaning forth,
smeared in half-snow, half-rain, November and the north.

* * *

Southward, downcountry
was where he lay
and I stood

in a loathsome mass of bleeding flowers
that April. Sun flashed and was gone, cold.
We two there, lashed stiff in old antagonism,

yet altered. It was that new smile
fingered on him, official, patented,
like the oil that shone on the pale oak catafalque:

such means they use to publicize, to promote
a marketable death.
He was worthy, worthy!—

I blurted, tried to blurt
in the clench of a surprise of tears.
And then my anger shifted from him to them.

In that horror
of hurting flowers
where I stood and he lay

I, frozen, was turned around inside my years
as a shadow turns
inside the changing day.

* * *

Why couldn't they let him be himself?
Like all our family he smiled
with a downturned mouth.

No doubt professional death-tenders are required,
competence is required, yet I wish they had let him
lie as he had fallen,

old Darwinist smiling
at the light gone down in the south,
at the leaf gone down.

Strangely, the birds had come. Already
in cold twilight robins sang,
and he heard them, the simple but rich song,

like Blake's, melodious for a fair season to come,
he heard them and he fell down,
unable to last till summer.

It was a reversal.
At the wrong time, in April, light dwindled
and the leaf fell down.

But hearts burst any time.
He took it smiling
with a downturned mouth.

* * *

The old Socialist!
And his father before him.
Era of eyeshades, rolltops, late tracks in a snowy street,

a flare of shots maybe in the dark,
and the talk, talk: that man eating,
this man not.

It was all so blessedly simple.
Hate, hate the monopolists!
Ah, and have I not, sirrah?——

but power of money has bought the power of heart,
monopoly eats the word, eats thought, desire,
your old companions now in the thick of it, eating—

is that betrayal? They fatten, but for my part
old hatred deepens,
deepening as monopoly deepens,

until my socialism has driven me to the sociality
of trees, snow, rocks, the north—solitude.
Strange outcome. Like so many.

I'll walk now; the woody meadow,
the firs, the brook, then higher to the birches.
I wish you were coming too.

* * *

"Alyosha left his father's house
feeling more depressed and
crushed in spirit

than when he entered it..." I walk,
going at last nowhere
in the snow and rain

that lock in air
and nap the gray rock with gray fur.
Beside me, among the ferns that confide

their green trust to the snow,
something stalks, or seems to stalk. A partridge?
Or my mind's shadow? Minute fires flow

in the lichened rock, and a yellow eye
blinks like a shuttered lens among the ferns.
Shadows and strange fires,

who can deny them, aspects of the cold world
and the father's house? We rebel
backward, ever backward, going

behind the ancestral impositions of reality.
To seek, to find—not to impose. So we say.
But it is a sad business.

* * *

Once he brought
to his blue house in the guttering chestnut forest—
oh, I remember this—

a pomegranate in his pocket.
But let me describe to you a killed chestnut tree.
Leaves, fruit, even the bark have long fallen

to the dark alien disease, and at last
the tree itself lies down
in a twisted, rising-and-falling

shape, and it never rots.
The smooth wood, pale and intense,
undulates

in a kind of serpentine passivity
among waves of witch hazel and dogwood
that wash along it

summer after summer after summer.
And so the killed chestnut has become
something everlasting in the woods,

like Yggdrasill. Tradition is not convention.
Tradition is always unexpected,
like the taste of the pomegranate, so sweet.

* * *

I must complete my turning.
With purpose, very coolly, I raise my vision,
snipping

a thread of the net that holds
everything together.
My splashing fears subside about my knees.

How easy! I wonder why
I took so long, learning
that to destroy

what could never be either right or wrong,
this net, this mere order
or any order,

is no real destruction—
look, I walk as I have always walked,
one foot in front of the other foot.

The rocks and birches take so warmly
to the purity of their restoration. I see this.
I have done it with one gesture, like that.

I walk in the tact of the ultimate rebel
graduated from conspiracy,
free, truly free, in the wonder of uncreation.

* * *

Well, the traditions of woods are sweet,
but something is withheld, something...
O my father, where is the real monopolist?

Can I, alien, avoid spreading
my dark disease? But you would say then,
seek its purity, deep at the root, radically.

If the orderly massacre of order creates an order,
then let it be new, even now, from the beginnings of things.
I am cold to my bones, my red hand clings

like a wind-plastered leaf to a white bole of birch,
the sky is speckled with snow-flecks
driven downwind, vanishing. It is all a song

vanishing down the wind, like snow,
like the last leaves of the birch
spinning away in harsh beauty. The hardhack,

clotted with snow, bends and rattles,
a sound like jeering in the driven twilight.
Why must the song be so intricate? What am I now,

what is my sorrow, has it not spun away?
Your face, snow-flecked, seems torn
downwind like the song of birch leaves.

* * *

Confused darkness turns a page. Wind slackens,
cold night is beginning, in the last light
the god of winter walks, gray and alone,

Odin, Windigo, Saint Malachy, someone
with a downturned smile brushing the fir boughs,
shaking the dead reeds and ferns.

Snow thickens, leaning toward the south.
Could he come home tonight
to his house, his woods, the snow, the snow-light?

My thought sings into snow, vanishing.
At least I have two clear choices: to stamp
in deepening cold, half-blind, dragging

my feet in freezing ferns, determining
my way in darkness, to the ragged meadow,
the shack with the rusty stove;

or to stay where I am in the rustle of snow
while my beard clots and whitens
and the world recedes into old purity

and the snow opens at last to the stars
that will glisten like silent histories breaking
over a silent face, smiling and cold.

* * *

O thou quiet northern snow
reaching southward wave on wave,
southward to the land below,
billow gently on his grave.

Snowy owl that glides alone,
softly go, defend his rest;
buntings, whirl around his stone
softly, thou the wintriest.

Gently, softly, o my kind,
snow and wind and driven leaf,
take him, teach my rebel mind
trust at last in this cold grief.

The Clay Hill Anthology (1970)

haiku

Let my snow-tracks lead
on, on. Let them, where they stop,
stop. There, in mid-field.

From Snow and Rock, from Chaos (1973)

Moon

From Clay Hill, high,
next to the old pitched cultivation
of the settlers' graveyard, I watch you,
eastward of the mountain there
rising, your glowing fervent bronze, so full
though with one edge blurred
as if in sympathy with the settlers lying
half in the blurred
receding shadow of April's snow.
I watch you, alone and lonely,
both of us lonely, full of this late
fire. Then I descend once more
to the cove, to deepening snow and the house
that stands by the loud brook in freshet
under the hemlock bank, finding
my loves there, companionate and always
careful of me. And you
are hidden by banked black boughs,
as I am hidden by love.

                         Hours later
when the night has gone to frost
again, a reversion to winter,
I walk out onto the crusted snow
and there you are, high
in the winter sky again, so clear,

like a free flake in the stream
of stars. I have found you.
I lean to you in the depths
of cold and darkness, you always there
and yet often hidden, as I too
am where I am always, hidden.

Dark World (1974)

Poetical Abstracts

1. CHRONOLOGICAL

this moment/ 26th Sept/ snowdrops
blooming I suppose in Tasmania
& Zululand, and notes
of a nightingale sprawling like waterdrops
down a bright valley floor
in Anatolia, somewhere a gibbon cries,
a cold surf beats

somewhere

    all those possibilities once
calling,   and I knew
I would go, and now

              losses, losses

He said, "Memory, the rose of time." She said,
"Ach, my mother, that old whore, believe me."
The poet said, "Hear the word *poem* fraught
with time." And we listened, we heard it,
that's true, echoing, we listened courteously

to the undistinguishable roar like bees or stars
or a wailing in the loins. And the child said,
"Well, if it means all that to you, I will—

I'll pray for you. Is once a week enough?"
The bird said, "Look, look at my wailing
as it falls,   bright
    down the valley floor."
The old man said nothing.

    "Nothing."

            a mote wriggling in a sunbeam
that falls through a bay window
among geraniums between white muslin curtains
onto a faded title behind the parlor glass
Mr. Britling Sees It Through

            and the cat

2. METAPHYSICAL

    fascination
    o' jack-o'-lanterns

    round livid fruit already dulling
    sagging

    on an autumnal doorstep
    in a stone wind

    leaf-waste and the chill
    discussions of dust

    the light inside gleaming
    at all four windows of life

laughing
gusts of light

flickering, now guttering
and ah the darkness—but

it brightens and again
life quickens, comic

intelligence leaps out
a quirk on the dark until

it can leap no more
falls, the darkness

rushes in, tidal
over the smell

of snuffed wick and sweet
flesh overheated.

3. CLASSICAL

what the hen does
after
the axe falls

running like that
close to
the tilting ground

an athlete
pumping
spouting blood

one wouldn't say
it's her
most meaningful act

but what has she
ever
done more

winding down, toppling
wings crushed
meanwhile here's her head.

4. SCENIC

bank of fog
an immense

dreamt marine
creature flowing

amorphous down the ravine
of the long mountain

into the couloir
as into a hole

slow motion
massive, unstoppable

the universe
star by star

emptying into the keyhole
in the box of sorrow

known as my absurd
head.

5. METEOROLOGICAL

(for JL, fellow allergy-head)

is it that the weather implies an
enormous room in which it occurs?
a vast hall, for example. I see

this room dim & stonelike as if
king canute held court there, but
not directly, I see it in a mirror

or periscope which permits me to
observe weather at a distance, or
as if around a corner, and I do,

I see faint glowing rays of sun
superseded instantaneously by the
drizzling winds of storm, all in

the great distant room, so great
& distant that it seems not mere-
ly somewhere else but in another

time too, totally displaced; yet
I feel that weather, my nerves go
slack at the first hint of rain in

that wind or when the barometer on
that wall falls, and actually the
weather around the corner is more

like a chart or pictograph of my
state of mind, as if my feelings
were in king canute's fortress—

as of course they are. This is
what is meant by being a man, es-
pecially a poet, although no one

lives altogether out of canute's
clutches, I suppose. This tells
us why all rules of conduct such

as revolutionary slogans contain
their own criticism, o tempora,
and are haunted by irrelevance.

6. RHOPALOCERAL

When these two butterflies flutter upward toward the blue-white
agatine sky, defining in their dance of sex the loose twining rope
that gleams with vacancy in the sun, my eyes frankly sink back and
cannot climb with them: back to this end of the rope where the noose
coils, dangles, calls.

Peculiar glitter, as of something false, associated with all symmetry. These two perfectly inversive wings; so bright, so fair to see. And those figures there, man and man, a face intent upon the surface of the pool.

Once a white butterfly made mirror-dancing with a white duck feather floating down the brook. Did I imagine that?

Two small azure butterflies dancing in a pool of dust by the road; from hill to opposing hill two chainsaws dissenting.

Wide blue sky. How many hundreds of centuries have men thought this the mirror of earth, as if our niggling particularities could be so smoothed and fused, instead of the mirror of what lies under the earth? We on the surface are in between, caught in a mighty reverberation of nothingness, shaken. Superficies. Powerless to deflect the organ tone that riddles us.

These are strange butterflies, brown and blue with spots of ivory; strangeness attracting special notice. Why not? I look into their symmetry as into a huge dim hall hung with tapestries on either side. I see that my imagination is the mirror of what lies there, out there; a mirror put into me like a foreign object. My being suffers ana phylaxis and tries to expel the irritant, but without success. It is I who am alien, I who am excluded. Symmetry is the sign of irrelation and death.

The function of self-consciousness is to carry, I mean literally to transport, these butterflies of the nonself. Can one think of any other? It is enslavement, granted. Why am I unconsoled to hear that my burden is only a butterfly?

When I thought to escape them they danced just outside the open
window high over the city street, or rested opening and closing
on the windowsill. When I hoped to join them they teased my clutching
eyes across the country meadow, through the umbrageous woods.

Where am I? Not locus, but substantiation; not wherein nor whereon,
but whereof. The crystal of windowpane contains, transports, trans
mits. I am "in" the lens of my eye. I am the veriest point of
passage and reverberation.

O blue-brown-ivory twining upward into the wide sky, how marvelous
that you sustain my dead weight hanging here!

7. MAYBE POLITICAL

(for Deianira with love)

the shirt of fire has been cast down
but gouts of flame still puff like flowers
on crisp swollen flesh   napalm down
the knoll a smear of flowers   don't
for chrissakes *doan tip it*   we eased
the 40 gallon pot of boiling fat down
from the range where the iron fireman wheezed
across a sweaty floor out a door down
oh almost down the steps   *watch it*
smoking flowers bubbling in pig fat   what shit
said charley farley   gouts of leaves
left on the maples like flowers like little
whale oil lamps in the forest down

gloomy ways   smell of diesel   lights
for dead pumpkins   the shirt lies on the ground
annually and the flesh hurts   bones
the bare bones of winter coming   burning
hurting flesh in autumnal mass under
the smoke-film where greasy joan doth
keel the pot and the brook limps
from its hole in the ground   greasy brook
limping to the sea from stone to stone
annually eternally   maybe   the worldflesh
being everything   but not measure   mark
the time-distance on this imaginary line
where cities spread from points   benchmarks
set in stone brass numbers under smoking
light   stone metal mark number   reality
doth keel the potted joan mixing things
with thoughts fires with desires   who'd dare
end war tonight for end of pain is end
and end of perishing is more same   shirt
tattered and torn melting into the ground
who can look   oh turn these eyes around

8. INTROSPECTIONAL

      of the shadow cast by earth in the sun's light
      way way way far away away across

      the void

and of the shadow cast by earth in the light
of a far faint opposing star, cast
like a pin   in
the depths of the sun

rise & turn & sit down & raise my head
& smile   and the dog
raises his head

& howls

Words for My Daughter from the Asylum

Alas, that earth's mere measure strains our blood
And makes more airy still this parentage.
The bond is all pretending, and you sleep
When my affections leap
And gasp at old hope vainly in my night's cage.

Dear marvelous alien snippet, yes, you move
Like a down-raining cloud in my mind, a bird
Askim on low planes under lightning thought,
An alter-image caught
In gossamer seed, my most elusive word.

There must be some connection, more than mood,
The yearning wit of loneliness, and more
Than meets the law on that certificate.
Strangers do not create
Alliances so deep and dark and sore.

Yet we are strangers. I remember you
When you began, a subtle soft machine;
And you remember me, no, not at all;
Or maybe you recall
A vacancy where someone once was seen.

I can address you only in my mind,
Or, what's the same, in this untouching poem.
We are the faceless persons who exist

Airily, as a gist
Of love to twist the staid old loves of home.

Strangers we are, a father and a daughter,
This Hayden and this Martha. And this song,
Which turns so dark when I had meant it light,
Speaks not at all of right
And not at all, since they are dim, of wrong.

Distance that leaves me powerless to know you
Preserves you from my love, my hurt. You fare
Far from this room hidden in the cold north;
Nothing of me goes forth
To father you, lost daughter, but a prayer.

That some small wisdom always may endure
Amidst your weariness; that lovers may
Be kind to you; that beauty may arouse
You; that the crazy house
May never, never be your home: I pray.

Aura (1977)

Aura

All day the mountain
flared in blue
September air.

The valley lay stunned
by color,
autumn's maple-brightness.

Now twilight comes;
not dark but a moment's
clarity, so that brute

wonder drains
from my eyes, relieved
by the evening star,

there, calm, over
the horizon, a lucidity,
a lucency. That light, far

lavender, restores
distance
and measure,

and inside my skull I rise
tall and free again.
Then

the mountain, free too
in its subduing,
intercedes, a new presence now,

a sense given beyond
color, around and surrounding—
is it shadow, is it

a blue myth coming to be?
Ah, wonder gone, how
lovely this welcoming! I see,

see the new dimension, form
wavering into essence
and shimmering—oh!

so slightly!—back to
new form, while
the mountain looks at me.

Brothers, I Loved You All (1978)

Paragraphs

1

Begin right here. The Campground Road. Some calls it the
Hogback, but that's up higher. Down here's the river.
And there's Vermont, all ridge and valley
and all cockeyed—seem'z'o. Over
acrost is the hayth-o-land, Whiteface and all,
Madonna, Mansfield. Butternut's back here. And Baldy
Langdell's uncle's place was right there,
him that set his house as square
as his own square Yankee head afore he died   and Baldy
   died and old
Jimmy   and Hank Rago
King, Malcolm, Jackson and all—
   all in a breath of years.
                A cold wind,
                        old and cold,
sprung these waterdrops from a bare birch bough,
these lightdrops scattering to the edge
of a pool of darkness. Or say we could glimpse
   Vivaldi's parchment now,
his hand flinging down a bright arpeggio…

2

Keep going. *There's nothing else to do.* Past

the few farms remaining, Manchester's, Jones's.
Past brutishness new since last
I drove here, sliced stone,
eviscerated hills. And then the worst,
these superadded trailers, this prefab, damned fashion
out of Monterey or Bronxville, God knows where—
the national mean taking over. Or
the mean nationals.

             Keep going, Waterville
to Johnson. I'd have thought
(almost) this was too tough, they couldn't spoil it,
ridge and riverbottom, massed heights,
granitic Vermont.   But they've walked on Kailas
   and thrown
town dirt on snow-bright Sati,
   they've exulted
before Kali.   They've put their feet on the moon.

3

Ithiel Falls, below the Nazarene campground. A name
clinging to its old place. The falls were blown out
in a WPA so-called work program,
1934 I think, to avert
another flood like '27 that had been true bedlam,
death-night all over Vermont. Icy water, the flame
in the lungs. God!
            Yet the dynamite
was a fool's work, wasted. What

caused the flood was a jam in the fall's crest
where the old covered bridges,
floating loose on high water, came to rest,
creating a dam. But then the new bridges
that replaced them were ironwork. Could *they* float?
Ah, Ithiel Falls, lovely cascading down ferny ledges,
and I never saw it.

      Why were the falls blown out?

4

Why was the passenger pigeon exterminated?
     Sometimes
I dream of those bridges; downriver on the flood,
shapes in dark water, awash and lumbering.
Why did the beatitude
who shot the last otter in Otter Creek come home
bragging? I dream how they yawed and stumbled,
how they wallowed almost but not quite like the huge
Jurassic animals caught in the deluge.
Why were the braves castrated, the stretched squaws
bayoneted up their vaginas?
Bridges are only bridges, that's all, bumping along,
  spandrel and truss,
post, brace, beam—
       arks
of a minor people and a time too small for grief,
crunching, foundering, gone in the rain-drenched dark.
I grow old, my dreams are factual and brief.

5

Not night now. Dawn. Six o'clock, a November morning.
But raining still. I stop. In the blown falls the river
sinks on a long grade, curling
through the dogleg. I lower
my window. Rain hisses on the coarse snow remaining
from yesterday's freeze where broken stems of mullen
fence the ditch. A grove of popples,
grayish-green, is a drabness opposite,
with one stark white birch outstanding. A jay,
slanting tidily across the water
to a low branch, jeers as he goes. Way away,
way in the East, beyond our boarded-up
Nazarenes, the sun struggles in a fog.
                              Once at Walden
it was the "morning star" calling us to the order
of this world.
      Tell me   Henry David   are you still called?

6

The Lamoille River Valley otherwise known
as these objects jays trees snows that wont cohere
or where on the waters of darkness Apollyon
stalks to make this hour
dawn's awful madness in the Valley of Humiliation
and him the Angel of Death but Im no Christian
and first becomes last coherence fails

connections cherished 50 years and alls

lost no art more Ill write what I want how I want

dont bug me about my words

the vision is cold chaos and I need what warmth

my old mind knows I rub my beard

I crank my window closed but there there the Prince of Prose

Apollyon water-marcher his terrible swift regard

flinging look his icy pointed oldwords where he goes.

7

Arthritic gray snowlight hobbles down the valley westward.

It is day. Who also will choose my delusions and bring

my fears upon me? Engrafted words

I sing and sing and sing

upon blocky objects floating downriver, my days, while my godhood

ordains resolutions, a chaos of light, of flood,

a *catastrophe*. I turn the key, ram

the old truck in gear, and grind home

down the Campground Road toward the colorless, futile

dawn—past Farell's

up Stearn's Hill, past the Whiting Lot. More trailers,

earth crumbling and eroding visibly

beneath the snowcrust, pines and birches massacred. I feel

nothing but cold. I catch my reflection on the wet window, alone,

a face old and broken, hunched over Ixion's wheel.

8

the one called Next steps up
to the wall. a face detailed
and well remembered. but
my voice won't call
when i try it. stuck. i shut
my eyes. i hear the gunbolts
slide home. i open
my eyes. my hands
are missing. i reach.
i have nothing but wrists.
the face falls down. i retch.
the next one is called Next.
so dream after dream they keep
going. yet i'm sound awake.
the world has gone to sleep.

9

It was the custom of my tribe to be silent,
to think the song inwardly, tune and word
so beautiful they could be only held,
not sung; held and heard
in quietness while walking the end of the field
where birches make a grove, or standing by the rail
in back of the library in some northern
city, or in the long dream of a tower
of gothic stoniness; and always we were alone.

Yet sometimes two

heard it, two separately together. It could come

nearby in the shadow of a pine bough

on the snow, or high in the orchestral lights,

or maybe (this was our miracle) it would have no

intermediary—

         a suddenness,

                  indivisible, unvoiced.

10

"There was this girl   18, 19   and slight

the way they are in that country   (you know)   laying

by the others in the ditch   taking

the bullets

with her body/   with which she shielded

as best she could   both her little child

and her zillion-year-old grandmother"

                hic divisio

facta est inter Teutonicos et Latinos

Francos circa 843 a.d./

          or,

            ahi serva Italia

di dolore ostello—

Dante who made it all ours and even more terrible

than perhaps it was   eloquence

so grave and so sweet.

        "Her mouth was narrow

blood-choked/   we thought her eyes widened

more in incredulity than pain..."

Ahi

thou inn of sorrow.

11

Oh I loved you Pete Brown. And you were a brother
to me Joe Marsala. And you too sweet Billy Kyle.
You Sidney Bechet. And Benny Carter.
And Jo Jones. Cozy Cole.
Cootie Williams. Dicky Wells. Al Hall. Ben Webster.
Matty Matlock. Lou McGarity. Mel Powell. Fats Waller.
Freddie Green. Rex Stewart. Wilbur & Sid
de Paris. Russ Procope. And Sister Ida
Cox dont forget her. And Omar Simeon. Joe Smith.
Zutty Singleton. Charlie Shavers.
Specs Powell. Red Norvo. Vic Dickenson. J.C. Higginbotham.
Nappy Lamare. Earl Hines. Buck Clayton.
Roy Eldgridge. Pops Foster. Johnny Hodges. Ed Hall.
Art Tatum. Frankie Newton. Chu Berry. Billy Taylor.
And oh incomparable James P. Johnson.

Brothers I loved you all.

12

I was watching the telly not serious you know just looking
with my wife there too and feeling all right after a dinner
at home together for once with our own cooking
and afterwards a whisky for sipping

and I really was feeling all right   Almost shocking

when you consider my age (65) and my line of work

(political) but even in the Trouble

you forget sometimes/ you have to   The doorbell

sounded/ Jenny bringing that big memo

to sign for the early pickup

I opened   It was a hooded man with a pistol

He fired three times/ there was a terrific

thud and I stood there watching a huge wall subside

under the pendulum stroke of a ball   while my wife's hysterics

drifted down the street like a shower of rain/

                   And then I died.

13

_____

And the water/ the rising water

                   nothing like it

     for force

moving everywhere   embracing every obstacle

          as if it were love

                   carrying everything before it/

                   a miracle

of conversion

               See how it spreads out & across

the field

          making a nacreous sky-reflecting lake

                   where geese

                   in thousands

rest for four days

on the long journey to Hudson's Bay
Rills rivulets streams springs ditches pools
                        it's a watery world
all trace of the old order going fast/
                              it spills
                mud and the rich mould
    of its long astonishing suppuration
                        and then
it's over
        all at once the movement has come full
and everyone
        puts on shirts of bright triumphant green.

14

In filthy Puerto Rico lives a bird with no
legs and transparent wings, a somewhat small
bird whose flight is awkward and slow
yet it spends its whole
existence in flying. Luckily it knows how
to ride high currents above the eagles, hawks, crows
and all the preying host that seeks
its life continually. As long as it keeps
above them, soaring between them and the sun,
it cannot be seen, partly
because the predators are blinded by the exceeding shine
of brightness, partly because the heart
of the bird is the only thing that shows, a speck
in its transparency. High it flies, flies, flies, hungry and hurt,

until at last it falls on filthy Puerto Rico. And the name
    of this bird is blank.

15

"I am a fanatic lover of liberty, considering it
the unique condition in which intelligence, dignity,
and human happiness may develop and grow;
not the purely formal liberty
conceded, measured out, and regulated by the State,
an eternal lie which in reality represents
nothing more than the privilege
of some founded on the slavery
of the rest; not the individualistic, egotistic,
shabby and fictitious liberty
extolled by the school of J.J. Rousseau and the other
schools of bourgeois liberalism,
which gives us the would-be rights of all men
as embodied in a State that limits the rights of each—
an idea which leads inevitably to the reduction

16

of the rights of each to zero. No, I mean the only
kind of liberty that is worthy of the name,
liberty that consists in the full development
of all the material, intellectual, and moral
powers which lie hidden in every person; liberty
which knows no restrictions beyond those

determined by the laws

of our individual natures,

which cannot properly be regarded as restrictions

since they are not imposed,

but are immanent and inherent, forming

the very basis of our material, intellectual,

and moral being—they do not limit us, they are

the real and immediate conditions of our freedom"

—Thus, living light cast back from a burnt-out star.

17

RAVAGE, v.t. To lay waste; to subject

to depredations; to work havoc or devastation upon;

to sack; plunder; despoil. *Syn.*—

RAVAGE, DEVASTATE, SACK

agree in the idea of despoiling or laying waste.

Ravage emphasizes the idea of violence; *devastate,*

that of waste or ruin; *sack,*

that of plunder or pillage. One *ravages*

or *devastates* a country, one *sacks* a town.

Unquote.

                        Please/

distinctions are important. There's still one man

who chooses with care. Anyone who agrees

may love me or not, but those condemning

my methods never will.

                        Regard the breeze

how it plucks bright autumn leaves

　　　　　　　　　　one after another

　　　　　　　　　　　　　to expose the timber.

18

And so with paragraphics.

　　　　　　　　　　　　It was in summer

that lovely word chosen with care when I

first loved this valley where the river

was a curving ribbon of sky

lacing together the fields of every color

potatoes timothy mustard alfalfa clover

and purple widemarching corn. The farms

lay scattered in their places, a barn,

a house, fenced fields irregular. Their old

horse-drawn mowers

and manure spreaders rusted in the yards. Fold

within fold the darkening hills arose

toward glowing mountains. Here was a peacock, there

a Mongolian pheasant—no exotics, no more

than the useless horse or ox, for this was where

19

all things lay in nature, even the plastic flowers,

the flowering plastics,

　　　　　　　　　　　　the plastic farmers...

　　　　　　　　　　　　Wordsworth!

thou should'st be living in this hour:

Vermont hath need of thee/

                          Carruth

being at all events not up to it;

                       the ancient power

of that vision is gone.

                    Gone? Was I bemused? The scars

are not new, the macadam was here then,

half the forests lay in slashed ruin,

the river's blue was more likely not sky

but the paintworks in Hardwick

clearing its vats again. And yet

                      somehow

it was absorbed,   humanity sick

with greed, with loathing, somehow was taken in

by earth, water, mountain…

                  No more! The weak

have conquered and the valley is their domain,

20

ugly, evil, dying. The old soft lines,

knoll and glen, mountain and river, that held

the farms like poems curled in time,

have been ripped out,

              raveled,

wrenched apart. The connections gone. It was dynamite

did it

      more than chainsaws or the great Cats, but—

          ahi

                              it was men's minds
that did it!

                    In this town, Johnson,
some have sold their own and everyone's
birthright to the ravagers, on our east and our west,
and particularly these two:
André Tournailler (*Anglice,* Toenailer) and Jacob Blesh.
Yes, townsmen, friends, I name *you,*
Andy and Jake, against every rule of Yankee decorum,
I name you in your public guilt. Here and now.
Look, the trailer park, filling station, plastic ranches, the rural

21

slums par excellence that were your farms! And all
for a hot pocketful of dollars.
                              I don't say others
haven't done as much, Farrells, Hills,
Berrys, Lahouillers, Parkers,
and so on—the length of the valley, to Hyde Park, Morrisville,
Wolcott, Hardwick, or westward to Lake Champlain,
a shambles, ravaged, devastated, gone,
or going fast. All in the name
of "development." But good friends, where are your dollars
now? And who has profited?
Not farmers. Not (God knows) poets. None of us. The poor
play patsies again for mean-spirited
weaselly downcountry men, the capitalists, varmints,
come ravaging in our dooryard like the strange coyotes

come from the west.

    And your *best* is what you gave them,

        oh my friends—

            your lives, your farms.

22

Now tell me if we don't need a revolution! Black
is the color of my only flag/

            and of man's hope.

Will revolution bring the farms back?
Gone, gone. The only crop
this valley will grow now is the great landwrack,
breakage, erosion, garbage, trash, gimcrack.
We burn it. The stink trails in the air,
a long thin smoke of floating despair
down the time of our valley. Someday we will be free,
someday when it's too late.
It's true, the real revolutionary is one who can see
all dark ahead and behind, his fate
a need without a hope: the will to resist.
The State is universal, the Universe is a state.
Now ask me if I am really an anarchist.

23

Another hard, hard morning with a hard snow
Falling small and fast. It is eight below.
Yet the ash pail brims. I must go
Out to the garden and sow

This remnant of value where the beans will grow
Next summer maybe. The goddamned gods bestow
And men...

        are at best a paradigm
Sowing and reaping in the void of time.
Or say that one must do what one does as though
It might mean something, so—
Broadcasting ashes, swinging my shovel low,
Spreading this color that I don't know,
Dirty lavender, dirty pearl, row upon row,
Death upon death, "sowing the ashes," to and fro,
A *tour de force* in an abandoned studio.

24

And I was past caring   so many, too many men,
so many children/   body broken, slack
as the spirit   skin & bone
like a burlap sack
with a liter of rice in the bottom.

          No one
wants lugging that around,

          let the others run,
I said, and sat right down, there
where I was, and looked up into the air
to see it coming.

       And when it came (that spout
of flaming jelly)   I cursed
and then I made a great sound: no shriek, no shout,

more like an enormous croak—the worst
I had ever heard.

　　　　　　　　For once then　　　once　　　I knew
what I had done was the most
　　　　　　　　　　　and maybe the first
human thing I had ever been permitted to do.

25

Reading myself, old poems, their inside truth that was
(is, is!) crucial, tree stark in lightning glimpse, hidden
mostly by the storm: complexities,
modes, names, manners,　　　words laden
with terror. What true voice? Where? Humiliated, in throes
of vacillation, roundhead to cavalier to ivy league to smartass—
never who I was. Say it plain:
death/beauty, loneliness/love, wisdom/pain,
they the simple coordinates. Was it shameful
to be insane, or so grotesque
to wrench lucidity out of nowhere? Yet my call
came a whisper, my sentence an arabesque,
my song falsetto. Put the book back on the shelf.
Gone goodness. Dear mother, dead father, what burlesque
of feeling phonied us, that made you make me hate myself?

26

A day　　　very solid　　　February 12th, 1944
cheerless in New York City (while I kneedeep
elsewhere in historical war

was wrecking Beauty's sleep

and her long dream)

                    a day (blank, gray) at four

in the afternoon, overheated in the W.O.R.

Recording Studios. Gum wrappers and dust

and a stale smell. A day. The cast

was Albert Ammons, Lips Page, Vic Dickenson,

Don Byas, Israel

Crosby, and Big Sid Catlett. (*And* it was Abe Linkhorn's

birthday.) And Milt Gabler

presided over the glass with a nod, a sign. Ammons

counted off

                a-waaaaan,,,   *tu!*

       and went feeling

his way on the keys gently,

                    while Catlett summoned

27

the exact beat from—

       say from the sounding depths, the universe...

When Dickenson came on it was all established,

no guessing, and he started with a blur

as usual, smears, brays—Christ

the dirtiest noise imaginable

             belches, farts

                curses

but it was music

music now

            with Ammons trilling in counterpoise.
Byas next, meditative, soft/

            then Page
with that tone like the torn edge
of reality:

      and so the climax, long dying riffs—
groans, wild with pain—
and Crosby throbbing *and* Catlett riding stiff
yet it was music   music.

               (Man, doan

fall in that bag,

       you caint describe it.)

            Piano & drum,

Ammons & Catlett drove the others. *And* it was done
and they listened *and* heard themselves
   better than they were, for they had come

28

high above themselves. Above everything, flux, ooze,
loss, need, shame, improbability/   the awfulness
of gut-wrong,   sex-wrack,   horse & booze,
the whole goddamn mess,
And Gabler said "We'll press it"   and it was
   "Bottom Blues"
BOTTOM BLUES   five men knowing it well   blacks
   & jews
yet music, music   high

in the celebration of fear, strange joy
of pain: blown out, beaten out

                              a moment ecstatic
in the history
of creative mind *and* heart/   not singular, not the rarity
we think, but real and a glory
our human shining, shekinah...   Ah,
                         holy spirit, ninefold
I druther've bin a-settin there, supernumerary
cockroach i' th' corner, a-listenin, a listenin,,,,,,
     than be the Prazedint of the Wurrurld.

The Mythology of Dark and Light (1982)

The Final Version

It will come to be, but only when the myth
functionally ceases, of course. Dark and light.
Clear as black and white, or as day and night.
Folk wisdom always rhymes because what we call
wisdom is the mediating of opposites. Total
presence, total absence. All color, no color.
Remember, ours is the animal eye, not dark,
not light, but juice merely, merely transparency.
Further it is tempting to say that she, the painter,
sees from the dark toward the light and that he,
the poet, sees from the light toward the dark, but that
would be an oversimplification. Perhaps our trouble
is that we no longer can be satisfied
with oversimplification. One knows
such agonies, forceful conciliations! Kodály's
duo for light and dark (violin & cello, Op. 7)
(the agonies, too, of Heifetz and Piatigorsky), or
Vlaminck's *Bridge at Chatou* or that extraordinary
seizing-up of the soul in *The Road*. At all events
though we struggle, and know we must struggle,
to retain our relativism, our mediating belief,
the two absolutes are unassailable. All and nothing.
Hence they resolve dangerously into one. Sometimes
god, vindictive and helpless, or destination,
the all too unmetaphysical injustice; but
for us the myth is $E=MC^2$. Ever more difficult,

more dangerous, less satisfying, this human function
which we call consciousness. Trying to make
ends meet (and the solace of facetiae). No wonder
so many drop out. Can one blame them? Yet each
defection brings us nearer to loss of function,
the time before and after myth, called Chaos.
"Ah," they cry out, such dear people, she and he.
"How can we continue? It is too hard. Too hard..."

125

Princess, the poem is born and you have woken,
A world's undone.

And it is no easy thing,
With brave romance and conquest broken,
Still to love and sing;
The tapestry is unthreaded, lovesong's unspoken
Horror spills out.

Yet you in yourself betoken
Love's amending, for you are Rose Marie,
Pure in transcendent being, free
From history, though the Dornröschen is keeping
Your beauty for us forever.

The sun
Will rise on the snowy firs and set on the sleeping
Lavender mountain as always, and no one
Will possess or command or defile you where you belong,
Here in the authentic world.

The work is done.
My name is Hayden and I have made this song.

If You Call This Cry A Song (1983)

The Cowshed Blues

> *Exsurge, gloria mea;*
> *exsurge, psalterium et cithara*

INTRO

    Intent in the
    night in the
    cone of light
       writing

VAMP

    Or what's called
      writing
  though words must come
  throb by throb
        through the membrane
  of the great black drum

16 BAR THEME

    It was a cowshed when he took it
    a one-cow barn beside a brook
    in a cove of alder and birch

floor of plank and rank urine, the wooden
stanchel worn in a cow's long wintertimes
heavy with animal woe

in the back wall
was a hole
with a board flap
hinged on a harness strap

where they shoveled through
the manure
onto the manure pile
once in a while

so he made a window where the hole was
a table and a stove, and sought the grace
words give for love in a writing place

PIANO SEGUE

Light on the page and all else
the raging dark

12 BAR THEME

And tonight the shed rides free and the cove
its alders and birches
falls downward among the stars

because intensity does this, a mind
out of time, out of place—
body a field of forgotten wars

and making does this, the breakthrough
to a great beat throbbing
in a place without place

o moment, moment pure
he is an undetermined existence
part of eternity, gone in inner space.

STOP-TIME CHORUS, TROMBONE

Soaring
 on the modes
 of sound
the modulations

moving
 over and through
 the pulses
of his love

known by no name now
 although
 a muse of everlasting
voluptuousness is aware of him

and the particular
 tones follow

one another
freely inexorably

SCAT CHORUS

    Cow now . starflow . the slow
    beat . over and over . flies .
    ow . the cords . the blood
    urine and dung . how
    flying . chains in the neck of
    Hathor . perpetual beating .
    her womb . beating . hot eyes .
    now . beating . a great flying .
    and pain . and beating . now

TWO CHORUSES AD LIB, TRUMPET

    What our people have never known
    but always felt
    in the mystery of the word

    is a force
    contained but not expressed
    spoken and unexplained—

    for meaning falls away
    as the stars in their spirals
    fall from the void of creation

    how simple and how necessary
    this discipline! which is the

moment added to moment of being

movement added to movement
notes in the throat of the horn
being and being and being

dying, born   and he
is alone, free
creator of what he cannot help but be

VAMP, GUITAR AND BASS

"Holiness," he says
   hearing an unexpected
modulation:
          at the point of flow
always this beat, this beat
   repeated
instant of everything he knows
   now   forever   existing   here
it must
   be holiness

OUT-CHORUS

And blues is also
   a crying in the night
exhaustion, constriction
   in the cone of light

and he looks up sighing
　　to the dark glass
where looking back at him
　　is his father's face

STOP-TIME BRIDGE, CLARINET

　All's fallen back
　　back
　collapsing into time
　　time
　the beat　　　of the great drum　　　is going
　　going
　in the wind in the trees
　　in the wind in the trees

RIDE OUT, HALF-TIME

　It is　　　his face now
　his own　　　his
　　and old in a moment
　　miseries, histories

　his and his father's
　reflected　　　little things
　　among others of this earth
　　the alders and the birch

TAG, DRUMS

But the beat remains
the moment of purity somewhere
poised on its long
flow   far out, far in

TUTTI

or on this page fallen
        notations   of remembered song.

Shake, Well Before Using

That guy three lots down on the oth-
    er side? Name of Crawford,
but I don't know him. Now ain't that
    a bomb, eight years we ord-

er our *Herald* from the same pap-
    erboy and ain't even
shook hands, but like I say he's got
    this smokebush, see, a ten-

footer, maybe more, it's what I
    mean big, right there in his
front yard, a beaut, take a dekko
    next time your business

brings you round here by daylight, it
    looks real fancy and high-
tone, like this bozo Crawford's pour-
    ing dollars on it, ni-

trogen and potash and all that,
    which he no doubt is, you
know what I mean, but the only
    bitch I got is long a-

bout this time every year, the last
    week in August, them
things, whatever they are, them bunch-
    es, like they say resem-

ble smoke, see, them little smokers,
    they bust off and the wind
blows them every whichway over
    the whole street like some thinned-

down leftovers from the sixty-
    nine drought, they make me
think of five years ago I was
    doing maybe thirty-

five down Rt. 54 in New
    Mexico hauling the
old Winnebago into a
    headwind like standing a-

bout twenty yards behind a B-
    52 when she lets
loose, you know what I mean, pedal
    to the floor and it gets

you thirty-five per, and then these
    big tumbleweeds coming
at me from two o'clock like boul-
    ders spinning and looping,

and when the first one hit I sure
     ducked down, believe me, on-
ly of course they don't weigh nothing
     and it just bounced off, moan-

ing like as it went by. Well, these
     little smokers, they can't
compare for size, but when they come
     fast at you, hundreds, slant-

wise across the street, dry-sounding,
     you'll take note. No question,
believe me. O.k., I wouldn't
     tell it to everyone,

but days like this, windy, it sort
     of feels like the end of
the world, all them stiff dead gray things
     blowing loose just above

the asphalt, drifting like some kind
     of ghosts with that scratchy
sound. Can't you hear it right now ev-
     en at night? You ask me,

it's one hell of a scary sound.
     Ora pro nobis, that's
what we used to say. *Ave Ma-*
     ria. Hissing like rats'

feet, like them smokers—that's the sound.
    Didn't mean much then, what's
it now? Who's Mary? Priests whisper-
    ing and me with the hots

for Mary two blocks down, but I
    sure didn't want her pray-
ing for me, no sir, you said it.
    And now I'm too old. May-

be the world's too old, we're all go-
    ing over the hill, you
think that's it, like together? Well,
    I pray, damned right I do,

what else with all them smokers tum-
    bling like New Mexico,
reminding me. Soon it'll be
    the dead leaves. Then the snow.

What a mishmash—the suburbs! You
    know it. So I pray for
Crawford, the street, the smokebush, the
    works. I pray for no more

Reagan. Well, you got to keep your
    wig on, you can't give in
to the dead. So what if it don't
    mean much? It means something.

No Supervening Thought of Grace

for Galway

My true friend's poems about aging and death held my mind as in a
      sea-surge
this afternoon, for they are true poems, and good ones,
and I myself feel weakened much of the time now from the nights of
      death-laden insomnia,
which no weakness cures.
Almost equinox. A cold March day in Saratoga with hesitating rain
      in the pines.
Beyond the woods, rushing cars and trucks on the interstate
make a sound of continual rising and falling, almost like a seething
      sea,
which is almost like the sound of my friend's poems.
But he is five or six years younger than I, what does he know?
What does anyone know? Here, here is where it is, here in my own
      skull.
Well soon enough he will learn. And so will everyone.
I went out walking in the woods with my hands in my pockets,
thinking and brooding, because like the sea trees are important, and
      rain is important,
and the important wet brown needles were springy beneath my feet
that nevertheless went falteringly, cautious for the litter of downed
      limbs,
the boneyard of the pines.
I found a half-buried old wax-paper Dixie cup

almost like a fungus, stained softly gray in a flocky pattern edged
      with coral and orange. Sometimes one doesn't care
any longer about oneself, but for a true five-or-six-year-younger
      friend
one would dash into the sea, if that would help,
one would beseech the gods.

Song: So Why Does This Dead Carnation

So why does this dead carnation hold
particular charm? Ten days ago
it was fresh, a bright, vibrant red,
but now has lost its gleam, and the fold
of its petals has loosened. It's like a flower
in a painting, or an ordinary imitation
in paper or cloth. One would have said
it is useless, yet I feel a kind of power.

Were they right, the Egyptians, to mummify
cadavers? I've pinned the carnation
upside down to my bulletin board
the way Kazuko used to pin roses, to let it
dry completely, I'm not sure why.
But I know my frightened mind can cower
to see my brown-spotted hand moving toward
uselessness, though it still has a kind of power.

From moment to moment the world becomes
memory, a still life, what the French
call *nature morte.* No embalmer
could make my hand lifelike for an hour
after it's gone. But I'll keep the dry
carnation anyway, the best I can do
to abstract our existence and wrench
from the useless past a kind of present power.

Moonset

The dark will come, I said,
soon now at moonset.

And I looked and looked to see
our night-lady

so grave and magnanimous
go away

over our hill, smiling
a moment, no more, through pointed

spruces; and the dark came,
the snow turned gray.

Yet then slowly the gray
was silver, the snow-clad

spruces began to sparkle,
and even the frost of the air

was illumined, a slow
mazy

dance of light-specks. I
looked overhead

to the stars, suddenly
so present, so much a part

of the night. The night,
I said, is all grave

and all a dance and never
dark. And on my slow

snowshoes I danced and skipped
gravely down the meadow.

Sonnets (1989)

63

But still, still...

        In stillness mystery calls,
though calling no one, being simply there,
somewhere I cannot tell, singing, not near,
not far, but song always, an ayre that falls
on my silence as if heard in the long halls
of eternity, of existence, this that I hear
in the incomprehensibility we share
and cannot speak, a touch, a glance that forestalls
the foreignness we felt before we came
into our knowing one another, yet no touch
nor glance in fact, nothing definable, no name
in materiality, only this singing, such
that together silently we hear and we belong
at last,

      always this sonetto, this little song...

Tell Me Again How the White Heron Rises and Flies Across the Nacreous River at Twilight Toward the Distant Islands (1989)

Mother

> *O thou great Nothing, thou Indifference,*
> *thou Forgetfulness, has not she in her own nature the right*
> *to be meaningless? To be what in their nature words*
> *cannot contain, the less than meaningless?*
> —Sadhu Jinri-Ghoramnya

(Margery Carruth, 1896–1981)

I. THE EVENT

Mother, now at last I must speak to you. The hour, so late but even so,
    has come.
Mother, after sixty-one and a half years of life,
After one and one-quarter years of your death,
After your incomprehensible durance and anguish, which deranges me still,
After the wordless years between us, our unutterable, constricted,
    strangling chaos,
After the long years of my private wrecked language, when my mind shook
    in the tempests of fear,
After everything between us is done and never to be undone, so that no
    speech matters,
Nevertheless I must speak.

The sea is not here, nor has it ever in my life been where I was,
Nor was it more than briefly ever in yours (you, bound inland, away from
    your desire),

Yet how you spoke, sixty percent aphasic as you were,

Of "the water" and "the ship," and of "the glittering water" or "the
golden shining water"

Between the ship and the pier when you looked down from the fantail

(Was she the *Vulcania?* I almost seem to remember),

How you spoke in the phantasmic childhood you were living again

Of the water gleaming, of your mother, of her leaping down into that
golden alley of death

(But she did not; she leapt from the sixteenth floor of a hotel on
Broadway),

How your pallid, brown-spotted, wrinkled, half-paralyzed countenance
grimaced,

So that I could not tell whether you were smiling or struck with terror,

Until I recognized that it was the ultimate human expression, the two
masks superimposed,

Mother, how you spoke then, giggling and whimpering, your voice
skipping from

node to node of your mind's dispersion,

How you mingled the water, the glimmering, the exhilaration of a
voyage beginning, the horror of a voyage ending

(Your mother, my Nana, the strange woman of glistening auburn hair),

How you spoke gave me to understand the as it seemed inhuman
human lucency

Of your half-dead mind,

And the way, intermingling there, these visions of childhood, death,
mother, and water

Were the wisdom beyond speech,

Were knowledge in its clearest configuration,

Which did not for one minutest part of an instant relieve your agony.

"O Hayden, take me home," you wailed, singing it out fully and
        tremulously.
But you thought home was England.

Was your damaged brain the same as a damaged soul?
I ask myself, and have asked in long, long sequences of perturbation and
        doubt
(I who have called and called to my own soul and never heard an answer),
You lay there three years, twisted,
Until your body became so rigid that no man could have been strong
        enough
To undo the knot, as no person, man or woman or even child,
Could penetrate your mind in its writhing, convulsive indagation.
Oh, the suffering! You in the focus of the pain of all our lives,
You on the threshold, knowing it clearly, peering into the darkness,
But so ravaged in the coils of thought that no current could be induced,
And thus you lay there smashed, a machine of random parts, of no
        definable function,
Unable to generate so much as the least beginning spark of an idea,
Unable to conceive any *suppositum* of your predicament,
And fear wailed out of you, unintelligible sentences that vanished in rising
        tremolo,
As if you were an animal somehow granted the power to know but not to
        think,
Or as if you were a philosopher suddenly deprived of every faculty except
Original fear and pathos. I cannot surmise a state of being more
        inconsonant
With human consciousness.
Oh, many as evil, many and many, God knows, but none essentially worse.

To which was added, of course, humiliation.
"I am not nice," you repeated in your weeping quaver. "I am not nice,"
Covered from head to foot with your own shit.

Once when I came you would not acknowledge me. Not even a flicker
       of your eyelid.
I thought you were dead.
I shook you as it seemed unmercifully and shouted next to your ear. I
       shouted.
At last, unmoving, you said in a quiet, perfectly normal voice, as in old
       times,
"I hear you."
Nothing more. After an hour I left.
Never have I heard anything more terrible than that "I hear you."

Three years. For you they could have been three million. You lived only
In the present moment,
The moment before death.
And the doctors who had "saved your life" would give you nothing.
Three million moments before death.
Should I have smuggled in marijuana for you? Heroin? I think I should.
A century ago the doctors would have fed you laudanum like sugar
       cubes,
Assuming you had lived through your first stroke. But you would not
       have.
You would have died quickly, appropriately, humanly.
For every technological advance, intelligence makes a moral regression.

Three million moments. Three million deaths. O my mother.
You lying there in a twisted, useless body.

You on the shore of death, perpetually.

You in the shadowy tumult of memories.

You in your language broken, stammering, whole aggregates of once-
luminous words blown out.

You nearly blind, your son's face unrecognizable.

You with your hearing still acute, able to distinguish voices.

You with your radio that the nurses always turned to a rock station, in
spite of your frowning.

You were unable to cover yourself, your withered cunt showing.

You wailing and wailing, no, not like a child, but in a voice torn and
wasted, a cruel parody of a child.

You with your teeth broken and rotted like barely discernible, almost
effaced lines of an ancient wooden sculpture (and the doctors
would permit no dentistry for fear the shock would "kill" you).

You there, always and forever there, in the termination that obliterates
everything else.

O my mother.

2. THE WATER

I think I know why in death's unrelenting moment you thought of the
water, the ship, and your mother,

And of your mother's death

("I think," so common, so perilous a verbal alibi),

For this is the technology of intellection in our time, state-of-the-art,

How are implanted in every childhood the great emblems of our being,
one way or another,

Then to roil fomenting like magma in our deepest centers, managing us
whether we will or no,

For did not the land rise from the sea? Oh, consider that spasm:

Did not you erupt from the amniotic fluid of your mother's uterus, as I
from yours?

That sea whose currents, swaying, are the flow of motherhood through
all our idea of time,

From the earliest parturition,

From the first warming of blood,

From the primeval rising and falling, the moist vapors and
condensations,

The warmth of the remote sun nevertheless occurring here on this stony
shore, this wall, this hospital,

And our returning through all existence to the tidal source, death in the
water and forgetting.

Once I sat on a bluff by the Susquehanna, that broad green fluvium,

I looked backward beyond the near diagonal slope to the broad field
undulating,

A farmer ploughing there, guiding the share in the furrows behind his
horse in the old way,

Patiently, steadily, a man familiar with the good way of loving,

And the field was writing in her correspondiveness,

But as if all the declensions of intelligence with its smeared graphia had
blurred my vision,

I could not see if she moved in pleasure or pain,

O rainlike sun, O earthen sea.

How was it when you were ploughed?

Not aphasia can be the cause why you never said

In all the clinging cries of your long death

The word for your husband.

O my mother, how we have in paltry intelligence made a foul language,
For do not we say "conceiving"
To mean both the transactions of love in nature and the negotiations
of thought in emptiness?

The land risen, streaming in all her vulval channels, the fecund mud,
The loam ploughed and harrowed (oh language of violence) and dark
and clean,
The corn sprouting, green leaflets, rows curving with the contours of
earth's body,
The worms working the soil and the swaggering crow lording and
eating,
Could you in the chaos of misery, the wound of your ancient sex
aroused and stinging under death's touch,
Make any conceiving of these conflicting emblems?
Or shall I say that before intelligence, pleasure and pain simply were,
and were one,
The undifferentiated sensing, without discrimination?
No. But for you were we all hagseed.
But for you.

When an old woman, staring blind, her skeleton, the skull and bones,
showing almost white
Beneath the mantle of her dissolving skin,
Dies at last,
We rejoice and say that she is a bride again, and we give her flowers,
Virgin of the sea, girl of the sun
—And mother, I could bide no more in these damnable
Inconsistencies, fear-wrought, flimsy, hysterical,

And I saw we are right to rejoice, a small, reluctant celebration of the
    drowned mind,

For the passage out of consciousness is at least in itself a minor
    advantage,

Though it is not a passage out of existence.

Ah, that it were, my mother!

Then would we have true marriages!

Rejoicing points our way through the little door at the back of the
    garden,

Hidden in the vine-leaves that we in all our power of thought are afraid
    to part.

To rejoice for death is to mourn existence,

As we do in the vine-covered depths of imagination,

All, secretly, all in vestigial instinct unknown to us, as animals who
    regard the world with scorn,

Look at them, great panthers, wolves, study those eyes, they hold our
    own ancestral, proud resentment,

Existence is the crime against the existing, and no matter who is the
    criminal

(The death of God, like the death of Hitler, is an affair of no
    consequence),

This thisness that is, all this something that could just as well be
    nothing,

The seed or the sequoia, the neutron or the galaxy,

What is and is and is and is and is,

Oh, in my rage at No One to address, I cry out: Intelligence

(For mind is implicit in it all),

Give over, it is enough, let existence subside,

All this that words point to meaninglessly like vanes jerked in the wind,

Sea, land, sun, consciousness, the universe, most meaningless word of
all (the fantastical converting into one),
I cry out for us all, Desist, give again the void, the one word that means
everything.

3. THE SHIP

Margery Tracy Barrow Dibb Thummell Sterling Carruth, you used to
rattle out
Your name like a litany, your Latin that nevertheless remained for you a
little charm,
You linked, you connected, a place for you in the generations of Old
England,
Yet you told me nothing of your family, you ran away from home when
you were sixteen,
A lost child whose kinship was the waifs, those Dickensian forlorn
whom everyone must love,
And only later did I learn that Tracy was the knight (the punk) who
inserted the stiletto (the shiv) into Thomas à Becket,
Or that Barrow was rector of Christ Church, tutor to Isaac Newton,
artificer of much of the *Principia*
(When first I read what John Aubrey wrote of him, I was as if swept
gently into an eddy of time by my admiration),
You in the long moment of death remembering your voyage (were they
two? I think so) to England
(And now my memory comes clearer, your vessel was the *Mauretania*),
How you crossed the shining water from earth to the great ship,
And went forth on the dark sea,
A child you were,
Then an old woman dying,
An event, an instant.

Clearly the first sailors were the dead. Why do I find here no scholars?

(Intelligence a structure of optimism, the human error, and thus ships
      must have carried corporate earnings to Thebes.)

The dead was placed on a dead tree at the riverside and sent on its
      voyage to the sea,

The temple of Osiris was built with a moated pool in the forecourt, on
      which voyaged a toy boat, the Ship of the Dead, wafted

This way and that by the currents of air that were Ra's whisperings,

And it is told that such a temple existed in Taunton, Massachusetts,
      which I believe,

For surely I am an Heliopolitan and Isis is my mother, and I dwell in
      the curse of Thoth forever

(And yet, You Jackal, Eater of Carrion, if words were inevitable in
      your numen, how more wondrously than the hieroglyphikos, the
      priest-writing?),

And all oceans run westward in our minds,

And if rivers appear not to, still we must cross them,

The ferry, shadow of the sun's barque, each sundown into the dying
      aureole,

A lingering, languishing disappearance (appearance in Dis).

I have seen the jet at 35,000 feet, a spark in the sunset, under Hesperus,
      infinitesimal,

And then no more,

The empty acorn cupule, vacancy so vast, turning in the rivulet.
      (Akran, Goth., fruit.)

Has anyone ever set foot aboard without a dark inarticulate knowledge
      of the true cargo?

The little last-minute hesitancy of embarkation.

Mother, I stood on the pier with you, in the turbulence of whirling
     images,
I leaned down to you, down to your words muffled by the wind,
I watched you cross, I waved to you, I smiled and took off my hat,
Little blonde girl frowning at the rail, your muff and shining black shoes,
The flowers crushed to your chest.

4. THE PHANTASMAGORIA

She shook him and the boy tumbled down the stairs, bouncing oddly
     from side to side. A box containing a loose weight.
At Hartford on the deck of the packet, awaiting departure, they sat under
     an awning and stared at the rainbow, one of which was located in
     the river halfway to the opposite shore.
The young woman, dressed in a long dark flannel skirt and a blouse
     buttoned at the throat with a wide white collar, held the
     reins with both hands, but lightly, as the carriage lurched up
     Hardscrabble Hill.
The dresser was painted, medium gray enamel, a white cloth with cross-
     stitched hem in blue thread, a large mirror behind, speckled in
     one corner where the silver had flaked. A hairbrush, comb, and
     handmirror of tarnished silver. In the middle of the cloth lay her
     favorite pendant, a blue moonstone very delicately carved to reveal
     the face within. Decades later it was presented to a granddaughter
     and now lies at the bottom of the Gulf of California off Isla San
     Marcos.
In the spring of 1926 she ran across a lawn, into an orchard, where apple
     petals fell thickly about her. She wore a short skirt, tennis shoes, a
     sweater, a double strand of amber beads. In the brightness her legs
     flashed whitely.

Her diary. Small black-covered record books, scores of them over the
decades. She wrote at a carved oval table in the corner of the
dining room, next to a fern and a telephone. For fifty years
she used a green Parker pen with a gold loop in the cap for
suspending it on a ribbon, though she never carried it that way.

When her first great-grandchild was born in 1970, she tried to feel glad,
but it was useless. She bitched and nagged as usual. No room for
great-grandchildren in her vision of the House of Reality.

At age four she stood on a piano stool in a white ruffled dress and
played a half-sized violin. The music was not preserved in
the photograph. Later one of her favorite recordings—she
had many—was Menuhin's performance of the concerto by
Mendelssohn.

At seven she dined at Delmonico's and marveled at the ballet girls
dancing overhead, their skirts whirling in circles above the glass
ceiling.

At thirty-three she went to bed for six months. "Pernicious anemia." It
was successful and from time to time thereafter she repeated it.

She and her two friends, Madge and Milicent, canned peaches all day,
filling the kitchen with steam. A cloying odor. This was in 1939.

In 1925 she refused to sleep any longer in the same bed with her husband.
She kept the white enameled, iron double bedstead for herself.
In 1928 she began refusing to accompany him on his Sunday
afternoon walks.

When her husband died, week after week she wept for his loss while she
watched baseball on the TV. "He was a good man," someone said.
"He was the only person who could comfort me in my trials," she
answered. It was true.

The assembly of skeletal crones in their wheelchairs near the nurses'
     station. The smell. The inosculation of thecal miseries. The wails
     and babblement. Death permeative. Dachau.

Her pride. Never to include the lack of money among her complaints.
     To keep her house orderly and clean; to cover up its shabbiness.
     In old age she implored and cajoled, that others might wash the
     windows.

Her fear of coal gas. How she ran to the cellar door to sniff. How she
     threw up the sashes when someone farted.

Over and over she read the novels of Arnold Bennet, H.G. Wells, Helen
     Hunt Jackson, H. Rider Haggard, W. Somerset Maugham, Hugh
     Walpole, etc. But when television came, she gave up reading.

In her first years of marriage she wrote stories for girls and sold them
     to a children's magazine. Then she lost interest. A few years later
     her husband gave up writing poetry, although he had enjoyed a
     modest success with light verse in the slicks.

When she was a girl she skated to school from 96th and Central Park
     West to (I believe) 83rd near Amsterdam. Sometimes, if the
     northeast wind were strong, she could coast the whole way.

She delighted in avocados exceedingly, and was put out with her family
     because no one would eat oysters. She regarded her marriage
     as a social, though perhaps not a cultural, catastrophe. She ate
     avocados standing at the kitchen cabinet and scraped the hulls
     with her spoon. She called them alligator pears.

Anemia. Miscarriage. Chronic psoriasis. Hemorrhoids. Gallstones.
     Chronic cystitis. Uterine cancer. Cataracts. Toothache. Many
     cerebral incidents. Rectal cancer. Two major strokes.

When was her finest hour? She does not know. She remembers only
     successive faint sensations of imprisonment and flight.

5. THE MOTHER

The Indo-European root *pha*, suggesting light and clarity, surfaces in
      phenomenon, the thing that appears,
And also in the Greek for "I say," *phemi*, thence in *phonation, verb, word*
(And I suspect, in *speech*, though my magic partridge is roosting in some
      other hemlock tonight),
For appearance is nothing until it has been spoken and written, nothing
      at all,
And now words are revenant, like the tides of shards drifting on the
      waste at Old Oraibe,
The issues my friends and I *settled* twenty years ago or thirty years ago
Are now impossible even to describe.

Nana, so remote, yet only second in the chain of motherhood
(My own grandchildren sending crayoned flowers as I sent mine to you),
You brushed your waist-long auburn hair until it shone as if it were
      burnished, you wore dead foxes with bright little eyes,
You came with trunks and hatboxes and bright packages of toys, and
      you stayed two days, and you departed,
You vanished into the train, which went away calling Who? Whoooo?
And you carried a book called *Science and Health*, which you left open
      upon the bed when you flumped from the hotel window,
And beyond you is no name, no woman, no mother, far down the valley
      of dark wind,
None in the mountain pass, none on the sunlit plain,
Far and far to the grove by the sea where dwells the water-woman whose
      beauty is too great to be looked upon
And where the bronzen child calls always in the sea-wind Who?
      Whoooo?

And the words are tokens, and the tokens are despair,

And the silence which is beyond everything, the silence which is
      around everywhere, is unattainable,

No death can reach it.

Hypocritical reader, you think you know better than I, and you do,

But your knowledge is of *tones*, not meanings; it is soothings and
      alarms,

The unrolling and rolling up

Of contrivance unending, images, blandishments, the calculus of
      inexperience in a thingless world,

The flat screen;

And your knowledge is the massive dictatorship that runs this camp of
      ignorance where I find myself;

Oh, the loathing with which I look out upon you, my horror, my
      despair.

6. THE SON

I held out my fingers while you burnt them with matches, one after
      another,

I snuggled close to you in the deserted railway station in Southbury
      while whirling snow filled the night,

I was astonished when you shrieked because you imagined I would
      marry the woman next door,

I never told you, when you visited me every week during the year
      and a half of my commitment, how grateful I was that you
      brought no other gifts,

I swallowed when you forced castor oil into my mouth for punishment,

I cooked dinner in the fear of mystery when you lay ill and called
  directions to me in your unrecognizable voice,
I ducked when you stroked the back of my head and told me I had the
  handsomest nape in the world,
I tried not to scream when you hit me with my father's strop,
I tried not to cry when you fed me junket and sweet custard with the
  half-sized silver spoon, those times when I had measles and
  rheumatic fever,
I ironed the pillow cases, towels, and handkerchiefs, you ironed the
  shirts and sheets,
I came to you in shame when I pissed in my pants at age twelve
  because I could hold it no longer,
I stared when you held the ether over my nose in a tea strainer so the
  doctor could cut out my tonsils on the dining table,
I wondered when you held my face with your palms and looked at me
  a long, long time until I cast down my eyes,
I was shocked when you laughed delightedly at the hot juice
  fountaining up from the cherry cobbler you had made and it
  spurted all over the linen,
I was sobered when you took me to school and explained everything to
  the teacher,
I never understood (how could I?) the hunger of your love, or why you
  called me selfish...

Often people ask me how you were as a mother, and I ask myself how
  I was as a son, but what shall I answer?
We were like no others.
I know this. Anything else is inconceivable. My mind will not think it.
But more I cannot say, for what created our difference is still unknown
  to me.

On the sea of motherhood and death you voyaged, waif of eternity,

You were the pioneer whether you knew it or not,

You were the unwitting pioneer, and most of the time unwilling,

You who for seventy years despised your stepfather, I am certain (in
      the nature of things) with justice,

You who knowingly first met your father when you were thirty,

The seedy businessman from St. Louis, that droll city,

You whose husband, loving and incapable, the knight in podgy
      armor, the poet from the land of the Brownies,

Talking away your blues with the wisdom he gave instead of love and
      that he himself could never use

(Oh, might I say, with the dicky bird, that things past redress are now
      with me past care!),

You, my mother, who taught me without words that no secret is
      better kept than the one everybody guesses,

I see you now in your eternal moment that has become mine,

You twisted, contorted, your agonized bones,

You whom I recognize forever, you in the double exposure,

You in the boat of your confinement lying,

Drifting on the sea as the currents and long winds take you,

Penitent for the crime committed against you, victim of your own
      innocence

(Existence is the crime against the existing),

Drifting, drifting in the uncaused universe that has no right to be.

Woodsmoke at 70

How it is never the same
but always changing. How
sometimes nevertheless
you recognize it. How you
see it from your window
plunging down, flattening
across the frozen lawn,
then rising in a wild
swirl and it's gone...

Scrambled Eggs and Whiskey

Scrambled eggs and whiskey
in the false-dawn light. Chicago,
a sweet town, bleak, God knows,
but sweet. Sometimes. And
weren't we fine tonight?
When Hank set up that limping
treble roll behind me
my horn just growled and I
thought my heart would burst.
And Brad M. pressing with the
soft stick, and Joe-Anne
singing low. Here we are now
in the White Tower, leaning
on one another, too tired
to go home. But don't say a word,
don't tell a soul, they wouldn't
understand, they couldn't, never
in a million years, how fine,
how magnificent we were
in that old club tonight.

Turning Back the Clocks

The old man had played twenty-one losing
    games of computer solitaire and he
        sighed, acknowledging

the constant twins, Defeat and Bad Luck, Castor
    and Pollux. He stretched his arms
        upward and then

immediately, abruptly doubled
    over in pain from the cramp
        like Hamlet's rapier

through the arras into his back, and a small
    rumbling moan rose from him
        like a bubble rising

from a farting frog. The end of October. Bare trees
    and snow coming, winter coming,
        snow and silence in his brain.

Time to turn back the clocks,
    he thought. First the computer,
        which was simple, and then

the clocks on the microwave
    and coffeemaker, and finally
        his watch, turning the hour hand

forward around the dial for eleven
    as he had been taught to do
        almost eight decades ago.

Shuffling in worn-out slippers, he went
    to the other room and the clock
        there. This is the only ritual left

to us in which all people, rich or poor,
    young or old, still participate equally, he
        thought. So simple.

The rich cannot control it. The powerful
    cannot exploit it. Nor
        can those in poverty be

envious. Slowly he climbed the stairs,
    easing his shoulder along the wall
        to keep from falling,

falling into awful calamity. He reset
    his bedside clock and crawled
        beneath the jumble of covers.

He listened to the little song sung by
    the October wind in the eaves
        above his head. I should be

content, he thought. And for a
    moment before he slept
        he thought he was.

A Few Dilapidated Arias

1

And thus the morning has descended. Slowly like
a tremulous lady down the great stairs of the East.
What I notice is language pressing in my mind,
surprising me, as in those times when I made poems
like sweet tarts cooling on the windowsill of a
studio in the woods. Day blooms, a somber flower
in our valley, nowhere and now there. Am I
merely misinterpreting some psychic blip?
Or has time changed? Casually the light extends.

2

So let the sentences unfold again, like a measuring rule
jerked into angled shapes that nevertheless trace
the line onward toward resolution. Let them be
a little sonorous, but only a little. And let them,
for my lady's sake—she who evokes this lingering passion
from hoar-faced hebetude—rise up in melopoeia,
plaintively, lovingly, or wonderingly, from time to time.

3

"Liberation" was the shibboleth and slogan
of my time. We even had a magazine by that
name, and now dear Dave Dellinger is dead.

So many have gone with him! And now who is free?
Only our depraved president, who is free to
send thousands and thousands to their slaughter, like calves
tumbling and jumping in the chute at the Chicago
stockyards, where the blood-scent overspreads the city.
And now we've bombed a wedding party in the desert
outside Baghdad! Can you believe it? Bright shreds of
the wedding tent flying away, bloody pieces of people
flying and flopping on the sand. Pieces of the lovely bride,
pieces of the groom, pieces of the attending elders,
pieces of children, musicians, drivers, and the religious
attendants. A bloodbath, truly. The desert wind rises.
The palm trees bow their heads, the desert birds fly
screaming. It is the absolute opposite of an oasis.

4

"Our crumbling civilization"—a phrase I have used often
during recent years, in letters to friends, even in
words for public print. And what does it mean? *Can*
a civilization crumble? At once appears the image
of an old slice of bread, stale and hard, green with mold,
shaped roughly like the northeastern United States, years
old or more, so hard and foul that even my pal Maxie,
the shepherd-husky cross who eats everything, won't
touch it. And it is crumbling, turning literally into
crumbs, as the millions of infinitesimal internal connecting
fibers sever and loosen. The dust trickles and seeps away.

5

Well, old Great-Grandfather Haidie don't know if he's cold
or hot, and dass de truff. Up with the windows! Down with the
thermostat! Oh my. And down with the windows
and up with the thermostat! Yes, yes, old Bess. Give me a broiled salmon
and a bottle of bubbly cru, cause we're goin' to be twistin' when
the wagon comes. And you know what kind of wagon I'm talkin'
about! A smooth ride, baby. Hell, you won't even know
you're coasting down the main to the cree-ma-tori-um!

6

"Day by day make it new," said Uncle Ezra, honoring
the ancient master known as Tching. And Ez wrote it
in Chinese on the side of his bathtub, which is where he
liked to do his studying, thus establishing
a precedent for his followers, like K. Rexroth and the
noble Sam of Port Townsend, my beneficent friend.
And indeed on all five of us the sun shone differently
every morning, and on the Emperor Wu too.

7

Now listen up. "Honeysuckle Rose." "Shimmy
Sha Wobble." "Ain't She Sweet." "Four or Five Times."
You hear? They're the silliest songs imaginable. No one
can sing them, no one. And yet... oh, what we did
with them in our great years! It's said that Penelope
wove her beautiful feelings into the worn-out shirts

of the worn-out suitors. It ain't the material, baby,
it's the quality of the imagination. How fortunate
we are to hear Armstrong, Jelly Roll, Omer, et al.,
on these wonderful recordings. Don't you for-
get it! Don't ever forget the soulful "Flat Foot Floogie."

8

The kind and so exquisite French lady who has
translated some of my poems into her language and
her voice has used a phrase that leaps out at me
from the typescript. "Une voix tremblotante," she
says, oh so decisively, so much more expressively
than anything in my mere American. Well, I
could have been born over there too if the gods had
only been paying attention. Fa-la-la, la-la-la, la-la-la.

9

What is the worst part of growing old? you ask.
Ok, my young friends and paltry scholars, I will
tell you. It's becoming incompetent. All my life
I was the epitome of competence; roughly speaking.
I could do anything—cut a hole in a pine plank
with a keyhole saw, for instance, or grind down
the valves of my pickup, or read government manuals,
or teach esthetic philosophy, or... you name it. In
the army sixty years ago I was called "a handy joe,"
which was probably the best compliment I've ever had.
And now? Other people must do everything for me

and for themselves too. I'm useless. Can you imagine it?
I might as well be a common amanita growing
beneath the tall, tall hemlocks in the dark.

10

Nota bene. My generation of Americans
is the last that can tell an ovenbird in the woods
by its little voice. This is a part of our knowledge. This
is a freaking datum. And when we go this knowledge
will go with us. Lost forever. Think of that. Then think
of all knowledge, beginning to end, and of how it will
go, an immense gasp, one of these old rainy days.

11

The guy who meets somebody on the street, offers
his hand, smiles, and says, "You're fine. How am I?"
is not as simpleminded as you might think. "Hi, Doug."

12

"After the malarial onslaughts of style, nevertheless
I returned to myself." Thus the distinguished visitor
from Hungary, Mr Ottó Orbán, as translated by my
pal, Bruce Berlind of the Lake Moraine Road. And
ain't it the truth! We had tons and tons of style—tons,
I say. Does anyone think we were too stupid to be
clever imitators? But the further truth, my dears,
is that we had only a small assortment of commonplace
ideas, from which we made the poetry that astonished

the world and caused the assembled young to utter shrieks
of joy. Was it a brilliant show? Or was it simply
a flop? Ah, now leave me be. I'm returning to myself.

13

Watching the U.S. Open. Watching the spectacu-
larly beautiful Maria Sharapova, her extraordinary
thighs, her seventeen-year-old angelic face, her sweet
breasts glancing when she bends. Fantasizing that I'm
twenty-five with a full head of hair and she has given me
the key to her hotel room—WOW! And then the announcer
says she is six feet tall. Six feet! Coll a p s e... Tell me, You
Geezers of the World, if I can pretend I'm twenty-five
with suave hair and smiling chops why, why can't I
be six-three for ten minutes? I can't. Figure me that.

14

Who loves the motes lost and wandering, spiraling
lazily, or darting with sudden agitation, in the last
ray of sunlight slanting into my woodshed on a Septem-
ber afternoon among the tiered cords of firewood, maple
and ash, that reach above my head—ten cords for my
winter's fuel—loves what the electronic talkers call
reality now, including this old ragamuffin poet who
leans in studious reminiscence here. And I love him.

15

Philharmonia is the country where I live,
the same country where Maestro Ludwig also lived
in 1820, when his deafness was "complete."
My deafness is the sort that comes when I recline
for an afternoon beneath the monumental spruce
of the northern forest, just as it came to me in the womb.
Because all things are music in my genial inmost ear,
and especially all things rendered in our unfailing language,
which is, as we say thankfully, our most abstract
medium, solely of our imagination. And in despite
of our rabble of tenderfoot wistful yearners let me declare
that the music of the heavens is never so grand or splendid
as the music of the earth. Just be still and listen.

16

Yes. Well then, old friend, since you ask, I'll tell you. Go
back ten months, to January, to the VA hospital
in Syracuse where I'm lying on a table, a surgeon
bending over me. She is an attractive and amiable
young woman, of whom I'm already rather fond. (You
know how I am about that.) She is removing a big, dark
cataract from my right eye. Then somehow her hand
slips, and the tiny scalpel damages me, causing
a hemorrhage inside my eye, though I still
don't know exactly what happened—or how. I know
a long time in a codger's life was spent in pain.
And in going back and forth for checkups in the snow.

When I told all this to the guy beside me at the Sportsman's
about a month ago, he said, "Why don't cha sue,
for Chrissake, you'd make a pile off the goddamned feds.
Maybe a million. Maybe five. If I was you
I'd be down to the lawyer's first thing tomorrow
morning. You bet your ass. You could go to old Paul
Noyes over to Sherrill. You know he'll treat you right."
Well, I thought about it. Believe me, I could make good
use of a million or two. And it isn't that I have any more
esteem for the feds than my pal at the bar. But it just seems
that suing would be the Ammurikan thing to do. And who
wants to be a stand-up Ammurikan these days? Not me.
Not I. Not anyone else I know in the whole Northeast.

17

Postscriptum. For now I frequently see in the low part
of my bad eye's field of vision an amorphous white
what-you-may-call-it fleeing leftward and into nowhere,
and each time immediately I think of Alice's rabbit
running across the green croquet field toward its hole.
Tell me, why is this? When I was a kid in the gloam
of Connecticut's dismal crepuscular bed-time I
hated that book more than any other. And I still do.

18

The sound of adolescence was for me no drumbeat
or the warm rhythmic slapping suck I came to know
years later, though somehow I knew even then that

other adolescents, those cruising by in the Model A with
catcalls and laughter, knew it well; no, it was the sound
of wind smacking the lanyard against the hollow flagpole
in the schoolyard next door to the Carruths' house all night
long. A low metallic booming. Vulcan's metronome
counting the hours of my insomniacal anguish. I ask you,
who could even masturbate to that sepulchral bonging?
Nobody, man. Nobody, nobody, nobody—that's who!

19

Species can be exterminated! The words convolved
like sluggish beasts in Darwin's mind while he pounded
his forehead with the thumb of his fist until his pain
reverberated through the night and his tears coursed into
his marshy beard. And we have *lived all our lives* in those
tears which have spoiled our view of Noah's joyful mountain
from our back porch. We have cast our eyes backward and in
for a long time. We have recited dim and dreary verses. Oh how
we have recited! And now the *Times,* the silly old *Times,* has
announced a new species. Yes, by George, and Jesus! Somewhere
in Africa, long ago, creatures much like us, but a lot
smaller, lived and did what they did. Who cares what they did?
They lived. And now their bones live too in their telling us of
their existence. Never say the earth is not extraordinary!
And you, little cousin, yes, you there, the one named Hayden,
reach out your finger, let us touch, ah—you from your
dark, vast, incredible lostness, and I likewise from mine.

20

When I stepped out one morning in crystalline November,
two great turkey buzzards, aka vultures, were circling
over my little hill, above my little woods. Their huge
wings made soundless, intersecting, comfortable circles
against the blue sky and fleecy clouds, very beautiful, very
simple and understandable, yet surprising too, unexpected.
Was something in my woods attracting them, some little
life, suffering, agonized, caught in awful physicality,
hoping to depart? For several years I've been unable
to walk in my woods, semi-hemi-demi invalidated
as I am. It is my greatest loss. And maybe the vultures
were watching me, a little slantwise, where I stood
by my back door, where the sun is gonna shine someday.
Leo, old Boppertop, alas is gone. But he would know.

21

I mind a time, 25 years ago, when I was standing
in my henhouse watching one of my old ladies lay
an egg. Well, she scratched the bedding and turned around four
times, then crouched and pushed, and crouched and pushed again,
and clucked and turned again, and said—so I could understand—
This is one fucking hellova big egg, boss. I sympathized,
but urged her on, with thoughts of a great breakfast bubbling
in my mind. She crouched and pushed again, a good old girl,
until at last she shivered and her comb turned white. An egg
dropped into the nest, and her comb turned red again. It was
a great egg indeed, a "jumbo" at the IGA without a doubt. I

told Geof about it next day, and he looked skeptically at the
sky. Carruth, he said, you're a crock. Worse, you're a projector
of idle fantasies, and he went home to his own henhouse and
watched his young New Hampshire reds lay eggs over
and over. Not one white comb, he said, amongst 'em.
Geof is a real pal, a true-blue from way back. For 25
years he's been kidding me about my hen. It ain't
possible, he says, and he lays it on about crazy old men
who see hens' combs turn white in their woolgathering
afternoons. I believe he even wrote a poem about it,
because he's a first-rate poet too when it comes to
meditating on mundane events. Keep it up, Geof.
Don't stop now. If you do I'll be hurt and disappointed.

22

Say you're the founder and director of a small arts
outfit. Maybe a dance company in Amarillo, or
an experimental theater in Buffalo, or an
avant-garde publisher in Bisbee. You have done
important work. You have a record of excellent
productions. The cognoscenti all agree you are
essential to the cultural health and well-being
of your city, state, nation, and even, many would say,
the world. But you are broke. That's natural. All artists
are almost always broke. You need nontaxable gifts
and grants from the big foundations. But in order to get them
you must be chartered as a corporation-not-for-profit,
and in order to be so chartered you must have a board
of directors. So you appoint a few sympathetic friends

and people who will help to raise subsidies. Then
the gifts come in, you keep working, and in a few years
you are doing better than ever with a significant record
of accomplishment and an enviable reputation. From
time to time new members are appointed to the board.
They become restless and then ambitious, and they begin
to interfere in your working programs. Before you know it,
they begin to organize against you and to conspire
with formerly loyal members of your staff. Dear friend,
this is the end. You have created something so good
that others want it. Before long your retirement is announced;
the coup has succeeded. Is this what we mean when we
speak of the "corporate takeover of America"? It is.
We're corrupted through and through by the capitalist
ethos with its blindness to everything but wealth and power.
We run like frightened mice every whichway, but we have
no place to go. You and tequila are living in Mexico.

23

"Go tell it on the mountain." The wilderness is around
us everywhere, of course, even on Christmas Eve '04,
but not on this mountain, bro. Don't tell anything. We
love the comfort of deer and fox, hemlock and holly, yes,
even the consolation of these lovely mouse-tracks on the
snow. We love our towering beech and maple, as much or
probably more than you love your pile of stones, your
nasty old cathedral. We celebrate the solstice with sap beer
and apple wine. We sing for this special season our hymns
spun from the bear-breath floating out that hole there in the snow.

What cheer could we have more than this as the days lengthen
at last? Pax vobiscum. Give me a little taste of that mincemeat.

24

Next time around, Jean said, meaning in our next
incarnations, your name will be on my dance card.
Here in Rhode Island at Stephen's on a snowy day in
March, this warms my heart, I think literally. Why not?
Sweet Jean, beautiful Jean, Jean of the blonde ringlets
and Celtic eyes, Jean whom I have loved from afar for more
than forty years, Jean of the beautiful poems signed with the
beautiful name, Jean Valentine, my dear, my darling.
Next time around, indeed. Dear Jean, you give me something
to look forward to in that bleak and dark hereafter which
we so disrelish in our happiness here on earth. Oh, Jean,
this is a paper kiss for you. More and warmer will come.
Yay! and Yah! Way to go, Jeannie Baby! I'll see you later.

25

Well, "yes, your metaphysician is a blind man hunting in a
dark room for a black hat, which does not exist." Thus saith
Prince Piotr Kropotkin on his first visit to the U.S. of A.
in 1897 when he dined with the gentility on Beacon Hill
and rapped with the students of Harvard in their rooms. He
spoke of "mutual aid," by which he meant cooperative
economics, and said he favored a federated organization of
society on the American model. He spoke to enthusiastic
audiences in Boston, New York, Chicago, and many smaller

cities, and was saddened by the obvious fact that many
came to see him because he was a prince, not because he
was a political philosopher. He became good friends
with Louis Agassiz and other American naturalists
and scientists, and was himself widely known for his
contributions to the theory of evolution, stressing
the cooperative rather than the competitive behavior
of animal species. He was a benevolent and gentle man,
whom we are pleased to acknowledge as an essential
contributor to the bright and happy heritage of our
American revolutionary thought. Let some other
names be added here in the roster: Johann Most, Ben
Tucker, Burnette Haskell, Al Parsons, Alex Berkman,
Mollie Steimer, Emma Goldman, and of course Nick
Sacco and Bart Vanzetti. Then in our time Paul Goodman,
Noam Chomsky, Denise Levertov, and me and my
friends. And many others, especially in these days
of imperialism in Iraq and the Bush tyranny. When
was it ever more obvious that evil is the State?

26

Month after month in New England and New York this winter
has been overcast, too warm, too wet, with occasional sleet
and not so occasional fog. What a disappointment! We call it
the Gray Winter, and so it will be known, I'm sure,
for many a dismal year to come. We have no snow,
the grass is sere and olive drab, the highway gleams
with water, crusts of ice trip the old woman who goes
out to scatter seeds for the birds. The Gray Winter,

so unprecedentedly hideous. No cleanliness. No
brightness. As old Bill said, the "winter of our discontent."
Otherwise, the beginning of cataclysmic GLOBAL
WARMING. Of this no doubt remains, whatever that stunted
throwback in the White House mumbles on television,
and the outcome is only too easy to imagine. Arrgh!
Remember me in your agony, my children. Think
of what I have foretold. I wrote these words for you.

LAST POEMS

After Television

I wonder continually about that time when we
Broke off from the other animals. What were we
Thinking, if anything? Were we trying to toss
All our aunts, uncles, and cousins into the
Dumpster in one grand renunciation? I wouldn't
Be surprised. And was that the moment when
Our centuries of egomania began? Oh, my dears,
The Bengal tiger, the biggest cat in the world,
Who was our friend and protector on the plain,
In the tall grass and under the squirmy trees,
Is now down to a population of only 400.
Where did all the others go? Of course we know.
We gave the command that drove them out. And then
So many, many thousands and thousands of other
Wonderful beings, whose minds and hearts we knew
In our earliest perceptions, knew and loved.
That knowledge and love tinge our thought
Today, and fill us with this inexhaustible sadness
Which we all acknowledge in our mumbling days
And which causes us to nod our heads slowly
And stupidly when moonlight shines on the water.

See You Tomorrow

Twilight is what the tittycrested romanticists say,
Referring to old age, Twilight! Don't they know
That things always get brighter, at least until
They become invisible. Look at the sky. Full
Of bright pains. And the earth, full of great
Flashing fears. Sparkling explosions are every-
Where. Highways run with the liquid fire
Of angst and hypochondria. Moonlight
On the cornfields mixes and flows like an
Immense sob. The next time you see a line
Of geezers shuffling toward the checkout
Remember they are entering the arcade of
Death. Flashing lights and crashing bells
Surround them, and the only darkness is
The space between the soles of their shoes
And the floor. Hup, atwo, athree, afour—
The slow march and the muffled drum. So
Never fear, they will get there in blinding
Dawn when the day of demolition has just
Begun. Whoop-de-do and tum-tum-tum,
Benighted night will never come.

"Après de ma blonde…"

It's over. You're lying there depleted, breathing
Hard. Then she says, "Oh God, Darling, that
Was wonderful." You begin to glow. Who else
Has such power to excite another's universe
Of thought and feeling?

                        Then you remember.
It was all caused by the brute of a
Boy who's always trying to get born!

Derailed

The old man with his snuff-colored cheeks and wispy white beard

is in this rich man's railroad car with its muslin half-curtains

and its plush overstuffed furniture, its polished brass fittings, that has

suddenly jumped the tracks and gone plummeting off into

the desert, careening, careering, dragging junipers with it, knocking

down paloverdes and chollas, scattering sand on the sky, and where

in the name of all the grand old divinities is he going? You don't

      know, I

don't know, and he sure as hell don't know neither! But he wonders

if a new big bang may not be coming soon.

For Wendell

For the light is changed.
For the song of the brook is
Changed. And we too are changed.
So select a pod and pick it.
Press it to make it split
And run your thumb along
The spine to gather the green
Peas and throw them into
Your mouth, and taste—
And taste the green spring!

Notes for new poem:

Since I was six nothing has moved me more than the spirit
Of the northern forest. Freya, Baldur, Eric, the shadows
Under the mighty spruce and hemlock, patches of snow gleaming
In moonlight. These were my dreams. I don't know why.
Then a lucky chain of events led me there. Led me to
Keene and to Chase and Russell, whose house might be the house
In Hansel and Gretel, deep in the green and quiet woods.
Finding a strange place where even so one feels at home is
Always a profound gratification. At once I was loquacious.
This was almost unknown, though sometimes in the presence
Of poets and artists with whom I can imagine a kind of
Half-hidden furtive collegiality it happens. Chase and Russell—
I love to say their names, which sound—don't they?—like something
Happening in the forest. We talked and talked of books.
Naturally, of Paris and the Caribbean, of music, the good old jazz,
Of how to cut down a hundred-foot fir tree on a slope
Or a fart-faced academic at a dead run on Main Street.
Of shoes and ships and ceiling wax and cabbages and kings.
What shall I say, dear Chase, dear Russell, except that in my
Old age you saved my life. Is this exorbitant? Perhaps.
But of style only, not substance, and at this point in
Our lives and in the world's, a little exorbitance of style
Is not a bad idea.

Poem No. X

What can an old poet do at the end of time
But scratch out nightmare verses in the old
Remembered measures that have endured
For centuries before him? How else may he
Memorialize these awful days and yet make
Due, if forlorn, acknowledgment of what he holds
To be the right and honor of all true men and
Women who remain in his tattered company
Of urchins and geniuses. How few they are,
Slipping away like shreds of mist on an April
Morning in Picardy or Oklahoma, yes! Good-
Bye, wherever you are, old friends and lovers.
Never shall we meet again. Our comity
Will drift among the stars forever, like
The little migrant sparrows of the plains.

What? Say Again, Please?

The calendar means nothing, as we know.
What dire divinity could distinguish
Between Monday and Tuesday? Yet now
The First of August looms in this disquieting
Time. What better day to signal the beginning
Of the end. And how comfortable it is, how
Comforting, to slip into the mode of
Superstition—yes, even when it portends
Apocalypse. Come, my dear, will you join me
In abandoning all responsibility, down to the
Last shred? The final shred? And then we will
Be gone. Some say that we are gone
Already, and who would deny them? Not you.
Not I. Pour me another taste of that Akwa Vitey,
Please, my dear. And here's to our comfort.

James Wright

This is much-belated thanks, Jim, for that
astonishing blurb you wrote for my book
years ago. As everyone knows I've written
ten thousand blurbs myself. I know blurbs.
When any human act combines great
intelligence with great style and great
friendship what could be more
memorable? I remember you, Jim.

A Vision of Now

Here we are, my dears, the autumn of twenty-o-five.
And it's very strange. The sultry summer lingers
Into October; the foliage that by now was always
Bright is drab and withered; and we are far
Too dry, except where hurricanes rage and floods
Carry off our houses. Is this then our last
Autumn? The radio is insisting, "Log on, log on."
And then the television pleading, "Log on now."
And signs and portents are everywhere, although
They are bewildering, because no one knows how
To interpret them. Persons of faith are tremulous
And unsure, while those of science apparently
Cannot read nature's peculiar new vocabulary.
Each of us is proceeding at a different pace,
Stumbling or running, aimless or headed straight
To a distant remembered door. The spendthrifts
Sing "Auld Lang Syne" and tip up goblets of fine
European brandy. Others are creeping and
Wandering, weeping and wondering. For we are
The new refugees, going nowhere. We are this
Old and horrifying, pitiful dream come true.

For Geof

I'm eighty-four now. Now I know what I
Should have done. After the war I should
Have stayed in the army. And now I'd be
A retired sergeant or captain with a pension
Much bigger than social security. Instead
All those years of puzzling with a stubby pen-
Cil over a dog-eared tablet of scrawly lines,
Synonyms listed in the margins and arrows flying
This way and that. Years, I say. Thinking
Of words, words, words, nothing but words
Zipping or fluttering above a cotton field
In the dull Louisiana of my consciousness.
And all the recompense was now and then
A moment's elation or a tipsy smile
From one passing female or another. Now
What have I left to do? Only this penta-
Metric shuffle in the checkout line with my
No Advantage Card clutched in my greasy hand
While Frank Sinatra is eating soup on the Muzak.
Give me a break, man. I'm doing the best I can.
Oops.

In Memoriam

Tobias Schneebaum, 1922–2005

He was an adventurous guy. Even at Yaddo
In Saratoga, playing charades, he would do things
That provoked the other players to speak in
Whispers and look out the corners of their eyes.
I'm not gay, he would say, I'm a homosexual.
He was also a Jew, an artist, and a gossip, a
Delightful guy. One time he found himself
At a Catholic mission on the edge of the great
Amazonian rainforest, entertaining the
Brothers with caricatures and naughty suggestions,
And someone told him of the Arakamas.
They lived in the jungle and were cannibals
Allegedly. Schneebaum's name was Theodore,
Which he disliked. He changed it to Tobias
And insisted on the full pronunciation. If
Anyone said Toby, he would frown and make
A gasping noise and throw up the window, waving
The bad air out. Tobias decided to go looking
For the Arakamas. He packed a small knapsack
And walked south along the river for many days
Until around a bend he saw the natives standing
On the farther shore. He stood on a sandbar and took
Off all his clothes. Then he held out his hands in
A friendly, half-supplicating gesture, and walked
Up to them. Months later he was still there,
Covered with paint, sleeping each night with a dozen

Lovers, eating human flesh to keep up his
Strength. Later he said it tasted like roast
Pork. And then he went to Borneo and did the
Same thing. Living in Asmat on the coast of
Irian Jaya, where he established a wonderful
Museum of native Indonesian art and
Culture. He began lecturing on cruise ships and
Back home in New York. He wrote books. He made
Drawings and paintings of native life. He became
Quite popular in our proud nation of armchair
Anthropologists. A documentary film was made,
Which was an ordeal for him. He wrote me letters
From New York and Peru, filled with acrimony
For the filmmakers and their absurd demands.
He was always in pain from his legs, and finally he
Was diagnosed with Parkinson's. He could no
Longer answer my letters. Then a few days ago
He died. I saw his obit in the *Times,* and I felt
A sort of deflating gasp in my lungs, and I knew
As I had not before how lonely this life has
Become and is becoming. Tobias is gone,
And the hurricanes rage. Please, somebody. Please.

[Fragment]

So strange. Watching the Indy 500 in 2005
And I'm 84. But at least I'm still alive—
More or less. Where are the pretty little cars
That Mr. A.J. Foyt Senior and

WHO ZAT AKNOCKIN

(at my doh)

Hey now, Pops, why doncha can

that hincty moaning 'n' Let's

Get   With   It!   Yes!

Yes, yes, man,

now you're cooking.

Steady, steady.

Red Beans and Rice!

Oh, you got that measure now!

NO MORE BASKETBALL!   Hey.

Hey now. Man—

Take It On Down.

(Yeah.)

The Last Piece of Chocolate

The last piece of chocolate
in the New Year's box
is yours, my dearest. Why?
you ask. Well, aside
from common courtesy
I think of two reasons.
First, because I've eaten
damn near all the rest,
but secondly because this
is the first day of twenty-
aught-six and you are still
with me. You are the most
faithful and loyal person
I have ever known, and the
most loving. I was born in
1921, a long time ago, and so
I am now an ancient of days,
a codger, a geezer, whom
no one ought to love. Yet.
Here you are. How extra-
ordinary! The great hero
of all lovers, Bertran de
Born, said that poets
must always make sacrifices
for their ladies fair. So
please, my dearest, take
the last piece of chocolate.

And be my love forever, as
I will be yours. With many
thanks for everything.

Valentine

Today, all day was Valentine's Day.
I watched the Olympic Games, especially
The Russian and Japanese skaters who were
Lovely beyond words, so young and strong.
The pain I've felt this whole day has
Thickened in my brain like an old baseball
Left out too long in the rain. How many
Valentine's verses have I written
In my seventy itinerant years of cobbling
Syntax and measure by the wayside with
My pack and my little trundle kit?
Hundreds no doubt and maybe more.
Then why am I so laggard now?
It's hard to say. Fatigue and old age
Might be the answer, yet I think not.
I was old when I was born,
And I've been tired all my life.
Even so, I think I've been
Reasonably productive. No,
The truth more likely is that I'm
Sunk in old anxiety and depression.
The verse will fail. The verse IS failing!
What could be clearer? Oh, my dearest,
You must help me again. Fetch me
My medicine and my imagination,
And then listen while I say in prose
you are more beautiful than any, more

talented and wise. You are my lifelong
love, my old companion, the one on
whom I rely to see me to my grave. You
are my beloved always and always. Please
be with me, talk to me, hold me, and stand
beside me, dearest, when I gaze out the
window.

Here you are, sweetheart, a most un-
conventional valentine, but only one day late.

Mark

You were the stalwart of our neighborhood,
Ready with a smile when we broke down
On the road. You gave us a jump-start on
Freezing mornings. And when an old thorn-tree
Needed to be taken out, you put on your old
Leather coat and climbed right in and cut. Then you
Trimmed the thorns with your axe in one hand
And you put the sticks in the supply of stovewood
In the garage, and all you asked for was a beer or
A cup of coffee. When you were laid off in the
Downsizing of Oneida Ltd, we could read the hardship
In your eyes, hardship for you and Laurie, but you
Didn't complain. "Everyone's in the same boat," you
Said, and you smiled and waved when you went by.
Your motorcycle was your best pal, and you knew
Every nut and bolt. You kept it in prime condition,
And often we saw you buffing the chrome, the fenders,
The tank when we drove by on summer evenings.
Mark, we miss you terribly. We always will. You
Held the door for your mother at the post office
And helped with yard chores or in the garden. Now
Nora must learn to live without you, which is
The hardest task any parent can ever face.
May God bless you, Mark, and may He someday
Tell us why He let this happen. Meanwhile we
Will keep your memory alive and clear
Until our own time comes. But now, so long,

Mark. It was truly great to know you, and
We shall never forget.

Q&A

What is a detective?

A person who detects, who is
Observant and discerning,
Who figures things out
And is said to be important.

     Ah, no wonder
    So many poets are addicted
    To detective novels
      From the drugstore.

[Untitled]

September, and the sky is grainy gray
here in New Jersey. The ocean is rumbling
along the shore. The leafless cherry tree
in this so-called front yard lifts itself in
silhouette, a comparatively interesting
image of the eastern wall of the world,
and from its midst, abruptly before dusk,
an arm of consciousness reaches out and
in its fist grasps the thought of death like a
wriggling crab. Taken aback, an old man
with a white wispy beard lowers his head
and nods, turns and murmurs to himself,
and then goes back indoors.

Sunday Afternoon

Trinity and Infinity and Concinnity
All in a row.
Oh, buckle down,
Winsocki, Buckle Down
And BLOW!

Who's Yer Muse?

They always ask, after the questions
About pens or pencils and which kind
Of writing tablet I prefer. No problem,
Ok? There she is, looking at me across
My table, this beautiful woman with two
Heads and three arms. Actually she is
Two women I know named Chase
And Joe-Anne. They are standing entwined
In a kind of backward embrace and wearing
Wigs, looking at me with mythic intensity.
It was a photograph taken in play at a
Dinner party, but I have been working
For a year in a kind of glow of love and
Intellectual warmth cast by her gaze across
My table. Isn't it true that the most moving
Images of natural art are always those
That occur foxily, without intention?

Card

Imagine a little silvery trickle of mercury
Moving around the gray and gentle bumps
And along the crevices of your brain. Gives you
The creeps, doesn't it. But it isn't so far off.
Just go out there twenty yards offshore and
The Atlantic Ocean is full of it. The halibut
Ground up and sold in a can will kill your cat
Just as it killed my Smudgie; the baby dolphins
Are born blind. This is the largest zone of
Pollution on the whole, entire earth. God knows
What monstrosities are occurring down in the depths.
But before long we may find out: crawling
Up on the boardwalk among the strolling hips
And bosoms. Ah, yes. A Merry Christmas to all.
And of course a Happy New Year too.

Financial Effrontery

Well, this is the kind of alliterative term I always enjoy.

And praise be to the muse, I just made it up

When I was thinking about my dental bills, going

All the way back to the 1920s when

My father was footing me for visits to the dentist

And he was as poor as I've always been—like

Piggery at the table and writing on margins it runs

In the family. And every time I've given the dentist

Two thousand dollars for my quotient of pain and repairs

He has come back to me for another two, for another

Quotient only two months later, towing me up and down

Main Street with his bills fluttering in his hand for my banker

And everyone else to see, and if this isn't effrontery I'll

Eat his drill and shit tooth enamel for two days in the

Courthouse men's for all to see and remember. Yes,

Remember me, Carruth the impoverished Luddite who

Stood up for us all against the Dentocrats in 2007.

You Can't Get Here from There

The day after this huge earthquake
In Hawaii two violets bloomed in
My ashpile, and not only that this
Is October. Two astronauts climbed
Outside their space capsule and
Nailed a sign to the portal saying
"2 rooms 4 rent." You think I've gone
Crazy. But no, no, can't you see?—it's you
Who have gone around the bend
Without the shadow of a doubt. How do
You like it here? Here where the track
Straightens and a light burns all night
In the room of the general admiral.

Poem maybe

On Margate sands I connect nothing with nothing
As our old pal Tom once remarked. These sands
Are damp and littered, not at all appealing,
Not like the soft sands of Manfredonia where the
Italian boys grew onions and garlic for their
Lunch. Can you imagine how much I wish I were
There? No, you cannot, my dears. Especially not
In the little time we have left to us.

[Poem]

The schlong is gone, my dear, my dear.
    Oh, the schlong is gone, my dear.
It has withered away
With the withering years,
    Oh yes, the schlong is gone,
And tell me, what shall a poor man do
For song, my dear,
For song, my dear, for song
    When the schlong is gone?

Dear Chase,[1]

Here's another for your slush folder if you want it.

Nota bene, however. This poem can't go forward without a revision.
The names of the two players I mentioned, Patrick Ewing and Zo
Mourning, must be deleted and other names substituted. Ewing and
Mourning are too famous and glamorous for my purpose. I need
two mid-rank players, tough guys, known to real fans but not to the
general public. In my mind's television I can see them, but I can't
remember their names.

Perhaps Russell can help, or someone on the staff.

---

1   Chase Twichell

Hey, Spike, Wait Up, Willya?

Wouldn't it be great to be Spike Lee? Black and handsome and rich
enough to sit in the front row at the Knicks game and talk jazzy
black talk with Patrick Ewing and Zo Mourning? Wow, that's the life,
i.e., the exact opposite of mine in every respect. Spike, I love you like
a brother, believe me. Without you I'd have nothing to dream about,
nothing to aspire to in the awful hours, even now in my extreme old
age. Spike, please make a couple more of your old rusty-dusty movies
before you go, and I hope they'll come out before I'm gone too. But,
man, if you want to make this deadline, you'd best get a move on,
and throw down plenty of that downtown Mountain Dew from the
cellars of Williamsburg while you're on your way.

H.C., Margate, 6/7/08

POEM/H.C./6/7/08

He was unsure
of his tonsure
but he knew damned well
he was a priest.
It was the Pope who didn't know.
But Woodrow regarded this
as a minor bureaucratic glitch
that the boys in the Vatican
would straighten out in due time.
What was Woodrow doing in
Las Vegas? Well, he fucked a monkey
from the Monkey Shop and he ate
a French-fried scorpion from
the Apache Hibachi. Wow,
Woodrow was living high
and having the time of his life.
But then the Pope found out
and he ratcheted up the
Papal Conspiracy and sent out
his orders to the city and the world,
urbi et orbi, and all the Catholic babes
went scurrying back
to the nunnery, and Woodrow right
behind them with his tail between his legs.
Poor Woodrow, every morning
for millennia still to come he would face the
same conundrum in the bathroom: how

to do what he had to do without
shitting on his own tail. And some of you also,
I believe, share this difficulty. There ain't
nothing to do, my dear, but grab your tail in both
hands and fling yourself down the toilet
as hard as you can, clicking the flusher
with your big toe on the way down.
As for Woodrow, you can look him up
in the Clarendon Ave Book of Saints and Martyrs
if you're so inclined.

ABOUT THE AUTHOR

In a career spanning six decades, Hayden Carruth served poetry in every conceivable capacity. His legacy includes forty books of poetry and criticism, a novel, and one of the most celebrated and influential anthologies of the last half of the last century, *The Voice That is Great Within Us.*

Carruth taught for many years in the Graduate Creative Writing Program at Syracuse University. He won the 1996 National Book Award for *Scrambled Eggs & Whiskey,* and his *Collected Shorter Poems, 1946-1991* received the 1992 National Book Critics Circle Award and a nomination for the National Book Award. He worked with James Laughlin and New Directions, and he served as the editor of *Poetry,* poetry editor of *Harper's,* and for twenty-five years an advisory editor of *The Hudson Review.* The Bollingen, Guggenheim, and Lannan Foundations, as well as the National Endowment for the Arts, awarded fellowships to Carruth, and he was presented with the Lenore Marshall/*The Nation* Award, the Paterson Poetry Prize, the Vermont Governor's Medal, the Carl Sandburg Award, the Whiting Award, and the Ruth Lily Prize.

He died in 2008 in Munnsville, New York.

Since 1972, Copper Canyon Press has fostered the work of emerging, established, and world-renowned poets for an expanding audience. The Press thrives with the generous patronage of readers, writers, booksellers, librarians, teachers, students, and funders—everyone who shares the belief that poetry is vital to language and living.

MAJOR SUPPORT HAS BEEN PROVIDED BY:

THE PAUL G. ALLEN FAMILY FOUNDATION

Lannan

THE MAURER FAMILY FOUNDATION

NATIONAL ENDOWMENT FOR THE ARTS

WASHINGTON STATE ARTS COMMISSION

The Paul G. Allen Family Foundation
Amazon.com
Anonymous
Arcadia Fund
John Branch
Diana and Jay Broze
Beroz Ferrell & The Point, LLC
Mimi Gardner Gates
Carolyn and Robert Hedin
Golden Lasso, LLC
Gull Industries, Inc.
on behalf of William and Ruth True
Lannan Foundation
Rhoady and Jeanne Marie Lee
Maurer Family Foundation
National Endowment for the Arts
New Mexico Community Foundation
Penny and Jerry Peabody
Joseph C. Roberts
Cynthia Lovelace Sears and Frank Buxton
Washington State Arts Commission
Charles and Barbara Wright

To learn more about underwriting Copper Canyon Press titles,
please call 360-385-4925 ext. 103

The Chinese character for poetry is made up of two parts:
"word" and "temple." It also serves as pressmark for
Copper Canyon Press.

The poems are set in Centaur.
Book design and composition by Phil Kovacevich.
Printed on archival-quality paper at McNaughton & Gunn, Inc.